STORYTELLING IN *KABUKI*

 Encapsulations: Critical Comics Studies

SERIES EDITORS
Martin Lund, Malmö University, Sweden
Julia Round, Bournemouth University, United Kingdom

EDITORIAL BOARD
Michelle Ann Abate, The Ohio State University
José Alaniz, University of Washington
Frederick Luis Aldama, The Ohio State University
Julian Chambliss, Michigan State University
Margaret Galvan, University of Florida
A. David Lewis, Massachusetts College of Pharmacy and Health Science
Jean-Matthieu Méon, University of Lorraine, France
Ann Miller, University of Leicester, United Kingdom
Elizabeth Nijdam, University of British Columbia, Canada
Barbara Postema, University of Groningen, Netherlands
Eszter Szép, Independent Researcher, Hungary
Carol Tilley, University of Illinois at Urbana-Champaign

Storytelling in *Kabuki*

An Exploration of Spatial Poetics of Comics

STEEN LEDET CHRISTIANSEN

UNIVERSITY OF NEBRASKA PRESS   LINCOLN

© 2024 by the Board of Regents of the University of Nebraska

All rights reserved

The University of Nebraska Press is part of a land-grant institution with campuses and programs on the past, present, and future homelands of the Pawnee, Ponca, Otoe-Missouria, Omaha, Dakota, Lakota, Kaw, Cheyenne, and Arapaho Peoples, as well as those of the relocated Ho-Chunk, Sac and Fox, and Iowa Peoples.

Publication of this volume was assisted by the Department of Culture and Learning, Aalborg University.

Library of Congress Cataloging-in-Publication Data
Names: Christiansen, Steen Ledet, author.
Title: Storytelling in Kabuki: an exploration of spatial poetics of comics / Steen Ledet Christiansen.
Description: Lincoln: University of Nebraska Press, [2024] | Series: Encapsulations: critical comics studies | Includes bibliographical references and index.
Identifiers: LCCN 2023027646
ISBN 9781496226686 (paperback)
ISBN 9781496239105 (epub)
ISBN 9781496239112 (pdf)
Subjects: LCSH: Mack, David, 1972– Kabuki. | Graphic novels—United States—History and criticism. | Space in comics. | Poetics. | BISAC: LITERARY CRITICISM / Comics & Graphic Novels | SOCIAL SCIENCE / Media Studies | LCGFT: Comics criticism
Classification: LCC PN6727.M218 K283 2024 | DDC 741.5/973—dc23/eng/20231114
LC record available at https://lccn.loc.gov/2023027646

Set in Minion Pro.

For Sandy

CONTENTS

List of Illustrations ix

Series Editors' Introduction xi

Acknowledgments xiii

Introduction: Let Us Space 1

1. Spatial Rhymes: Linkages and Refrains 25
2. Choreographies: Flows, Foldings, and Plasticities 52
3. Perspectives: Graphiation, Knots, and Positioning 85
4. Rhythms: Flow, Loops, and Coherence 123

Conclusion: It Opens at the Close 161

Notes 173

Bibliography 179

Index 183

ILLUSTRATIONS

1. *Kabuki: Circle of Blood*, act 2   15
2. *Kabuki: Skin Deep*, 84   28
3. *Kabuki: Skin Deep*, 54   64
4. *Kabuki: Skin Deep*, 41   70
5. *Kabuki: Dreams*, 309   78
6. *Kabuki: Skin Deep*, 65   98
7. *Kabuki: Metamorphosis*, 154   104
8. *Kabuki: Metamorphosis*, 178   108
9. *Kabuki: Circle of Blood*, 196   128
10. *Kabuki: Metamorphosis*, 288, and *Scarab: Lost in Translation*, 320   143

SERIES EDITORS' INTRODUCTION
Martin Lund and Julia Round

Space and spatial form are essential elements of comics storytelling. In *Storytelling in "Kabuki,"* Steen Christiansen explores how the various uses of space in David Mack's comic book *Kabuki* (1994–2007) can help us better understand the composition of comics. Comics scholarship has often tended to privilege analysis of the verbal, focusing on scripting, themes, narrative structures, and so forth. By contrast, Mack is primarily known as a comics artist. His use of visual tropes within his own storytelling can inform how we analyze artistic layout in comics more generally.

By exploring *Kabuki*'s treatment of space through four key concepts—rhyme, choreography, perspective, and rhythm—Christiansen effectively relates the visual layouts of the comics page to poetic tropes. The resulting concept of "spatial poetics" foregrounds the visual aspect of comics storytelling and emphasizes connections and correspondences on the page, while not denying the interplay between word and image or the narrative function of sequentiality. It thus has the potential to both fill a significant gap in comics studies and augment existing methods and theories.

The parallel that this book draws between comics storytelling and poetic structure also contributes to the wider landscape of media studies in a transmedial and multimodal world, where texts exist across many platforms and storytelling increasingly takes on visual forms. Christiansen's close focus on *Kabuki*, a popular and long-running comic that has received only limited scholarly attention to date, also speaks to the aims of this series.

In the creation of comics or graphic novels, "encapsulation" refers to the artistic and cognitive process whereby panels, images, words, and page layout create meaning and engage the reader. These connotations of selection and design underpin the aims of the series Encapsulations: Critical Comics Studies. Our series of short monographs offers close readings of carefully delineated bodies of comics work with an emphasis on expanding the critical range and depth of comics studies.

By looking at understudied and overlooked texts, artists, and publishers, Encapsulations facilitates a move away from the same "big" and oft-examined texts. Instead the series uses more diverse case studies to explore new and existing critical theories in tune with an interdisciplinary, intersectional, and global approach to comics scholarship. With an eye to breaking established patterns and forging new opportunities for scholarship, books in the series advance the theoretical grounding of comics scholarship and broaden critical knowledge of global comics. By showcasing new interdisciplinary perspectives and addressing emerging conceptual, formal, and methodological problems, Encapsulations promotes new approaches, contributes to the diversity of comics scholarship, and delves into uncharted sections of the comics archive.

Compact, affordable, and accessibly written, books in the Encapsulations series are addressed to the interested general reader as well as scholars and students. These volumes provide teachable, critical texts that foster a deeper general understanding of comics' cultural and historical impact, promote critical public literacy, and expand notions of what is worthy of academic study. We are excited to welcome *Kabuki* and its conceptualization of spatial poetics into the debate.

ACKNOWLEDGMENTS

A special thank you to series editors Julia Round and Martin Lund for making this book infinitely better.

Thank you also to Rikke Platz Cortsen for generously allowing me access to her magnificent dissertation. May it be published soon.

STORYTELLING IN *KABUKI*

Introduction

Let Us Space

Kabuki, by David Mack, tells a story that employs a wide range of comic book techniques. Comics' plastic nature allows Mack to weave together repeating events, dying dreams, bipolar hallucinations, and metafictional loops, along with thrilling science fiction action, martial arts fights, a love story, and the traumatic experience of losing a parent, into a coherent whole. *Kabuki* starts out as a relatively conventional comic book, but after the first collection Mack begins exploring the dynamic potentials of page layouts and panel relations across issues. The relatively straightforward premise of *Kabuki* as a science fiction action thriller comic is offset by its far more complex spatial arrangement. In this way, *Kabuki* presents a useful opportunity to explore how space functions in comics. Space should be understood as the spatial arrangements of comics' visual expression. As a visual medium, comics arrange components spatially to produce narrative, atmosphere, symbolic interaction, and many other patterns. Space is a core part of comics' visuality because comics' static nature means that everything they express must be expressed spatially. That spatial arrangement is key to understanding comics' visual hierarchy.

Comics capture relations of space in what I call spatial form; every part of the comics page is pregnant with aesthetic potentials, and comics must be understood as a relational practice that explores these potentials. As for defining comics, I agree with Kai Mikkonen that it is somewhat futile to search for a definition.[1] This is not because definitions are useless but because formal definitions tend to privilege one or another formal element of comics as the necessary one and disregard what Bart Beaty terms the "comics world," which are all the creators, practices, institutions, companies, readers, and so forth that participate in whatever is called comics at any given time.[2] As Beaty recognizes, formalist and functionalist definitions are part of this comics world, but there are no strict boundaries around it. Fuzzy logic and fuzzy sets blend what is thought of as comics, suggesting that any comics definition will also necessarily have a historical component.[3]

Still, as formalist (and minimalist) definitions go, I have a preference for Thierry Groensteen's "iconic solidarity," which interprets comics as "interdependent images . . . participating in a series," simultaneously separated and coexisting.[4] While few works meet that criterion, examples being comics that have a series without images (as in *Alpha Flight* issue 6, by John Byrne) or novels that employ interdependent images in a series (such as Mark Z. Danielewski's *The Fifty Year Sword*), Groensteen's definition speaks to something crucial for comics' expression. Although not explicit in Groensteen's definition, space is evident in both the independence and interdependence of images. There is some degree of sequential-spatial relation between images, and there is a series of these relations. While variations are many, we can argue that the phrase "interdependent images" speaks mainly to images on a single page and "participating in a series" speaks mainly to consecutive pages. Both dimensions of Groensteen's definition are part of comics' spatial form. Such a conception of comics includes notions of sequence, juxtaposition, and succession yet does not require them to always be present. Written text is also avoided as a necessary element, though it may certainly be present, which will inevitably mean spatially present.

Problematically, this current definition would not exclude painting, photography, and other visual arts. Yet this is the trajectory that Beaty traces; comics are not separate from other visual arts, except by definition. Mack often references painters in his works, borrowing and adopting their styles for briefer or longer stretches. He also uses photography and a host of other mixed-media practices in his comics. Scott Bukatman identifies an affinity between Mike Mignola and the sculptor Auguste Rodin and their rendition of bodies in stasis.[5] Comics as a medium are embroiled in art, and only historical contingencies have deemphasized this connection.

In any case, *Kabuki* is a comic. It tells a story through images and text, it was published by comics publishers, it was distributed by comics distributors, its creator worked in comics both before and after *Kabuki*, and it draws heavily on comics conventions, genres, and formulas, much more so than any other visual art. By whichever definition of comics chosen, *Kabuki* will be understood as a comic. For this book, I will remain within Groensteen's formalist-minimalist definition, in order to develop a spatial poetics of comics. Spatial poetics is understood here as the plurality of ways that comics employ the spatial arrangements of its visual aspects—layout, repeating motifs, and so forth—as well as the sequential spatiality of comics' narrative form.

The contribution of this book is thus not a clarification of what comics are but, instead, what comics can do, specifically what comics can do with space. Although it is a detailed study of one particular concluded comics series, the ideas developed here are certainly not limited to just this one comic or creator. What my emphasis on space, spatial form, and a new set of concepts can do is provide different insights into the poetics of comics, a concern that goes beyond any particular definition of comics.

I propose four main aspects of comics for understanding spatial form: (1) *rhymes*, understood as the way that specific motifs repeat across panels and pages, that is, in width, height, and depth; (2) *choreographies*, as the way that space and time exist as an interaction on the comics page and in series; (3) *perspectives*, as the way that spatial positioning impacts storytelling both as focalization and as reader positioning; and (4) *rhythms*, as the way information is arranged spatially across the page, sequence, or series. Each of these aspects will be elaborated on in the subsequent four chapters.

What Is *Kabuki*?

Kabuki is an American comic book series that ran from 1994 to 2007 and was written and illustrated by David Mack. Several collected editions and collectors' editions have kept the series present in comics culture after its conclusion. David Mack himself earned a BFA in graphic design from Northern Kentucky University, submitting the first volume of *Kabuki* as his final thesis. *Kabuki* has been his major comics work as both writer and artist. Although he has done more interior artwork, such as *Grendel: Black, White, and Red*, with Matt Fraction, he has turned to doing cover artwork for series, including *Alias*, *Justice League of America*, and *American Gods*. He has also written story arcs for *Daredevil*, including the introduction of the character Echo. His art has appeared in several TV shows, such as *Dexter*, *Jessica Jones*, and *Daredevil*, and he has done the opening titles for *Captain America: Winter Soldier*. He also illustrated the *Dexter: Dark Echo* webseries with Bill Sienkiewicz and worked with Neil Gaiman for covers for *Norse Mythology* and Gaiman's Neverwear clothing collection. Mack was nominated for the 2020 Eisner Award for Best Cover Artist for his work on *Fight Club 3* and *American Gods*. In other words, Mack has achieved both critical and commercial success, even as he remains overlooked in comics scholarship.

Mack's style has undergone an extensive expansion throughout his career. Starting out with relatively traditional black-and-white line art, color has slowly been added, as has a preponderance of collage-style techniques. His later work has turned increasingly to watercolor paintings, not only for his covers but also for the interior art of the later *Kabuki* collections. Especially after concluding *Kabuki*, Mack has also more clearly exhibited his inspirations from painters such as Gustav Klimt and Egon Schiele. The decorative style and technique of *Kabuki* always exhibited a Klimt inspiration, but the inspiration and impact have become steadily more apparent. There is not a clear-cut, linear evolution taking place here, since the collection *Dreams* was in a full-color, decorative style while Mack was producing a black-and-white drawing style in *Circle of Blood* at the same time. To some extent, Mack's style follows the story being told.

Kabuki is the story of losing a parent, the trauma that follows such an event, and the repetition of this trauma. Repeating the main event creates a narrative motif that most of the collected volumes circle. Narrative events are repeated from different character perspectives and from Kabuki's different mental states. Each new volume in the *Kabuki* series presents us with new story information and a new, different version of already illustrated events. The effect is one of narrative vertigo that culminates in a metafictional encounter between Kabuki and David Mack. Spatially, this vertiginous feeling is both stabilized and emphasized in two ways. First, panel compositions and page layouts repeat across collections. Small changes and recontextualizations alter past events, while also providing a degree of continuity between sometimes quite disparate stories. Second, the series increasingly departs from classic gridding techniques to rely more on splash pages. This means that the links between pages and events are at times highly tenuous and associative rather than narrative.

Currently, the best way to access the *Kabuki* story line is the four-volume set of omnibuses that include the main story line along with a host of extras from various sources. Throughout this book, I will reference this omnibus set as the standard edition. The first three omnibuses collect the *Kabuki* story line proper, with the fourth omnibus collecting the two spin-offs, *Masks of the Noh* and *Scarab*. While the three first omnibuses are chronological in terms of story and also mostly in terms of publication, the fourth omnibus collects story arcs across narrative and publication chronology. Unfortunately, these omnibus editions—like the original editions—are not paginated. The only solution for referencing has been to manually count pages, with splash pages counting as a single page. Hopefully my descriptions of events along with the inserted images will help orient the reader.

Everything begins with the one-shot volume *Fear the Reaper*, published as a stand-alone book in 1994 by Caliber Comics. It introduces the premise of *Kabuki*: Kabuki, whose real name is Ukiko, is part of the Noh, a secret government agency in future Japan. The Noh enforces a police state in Japan that balances crime and order in the most profitable way for the economy. This is done partly through violence and partly through entertainment. The Noh TV station serves up a mix of propaganda and fiction programming. The Noh agents' exploits and assassinations are fictionalized in a long-running animated series. This TV series is shown only minimally in *Fear the Reaper* but becomes significant later on, particularly in the spin-off *Scarab: Lost in Translation*. The Noh is led by General Kai, who personally oversees Noh agents Kabuki, Scarab, Tigerlily, Siamese (twin assassins who work as one unit), Ice, Snapdragon, and

Butoh. The Noh fight the Kai Syndicate, led by Ryuichi Kai, the son of General Kai.

Other than providing background, *Fear the Reaper* is a story of Kabuki killing a crime boss in a technology-saturated future Japan. Genre-wise, this identifies *Kabuki* as a cyberpunk-styled action comic that would fit alongside Tsutomo Nieh's *Blame!* (1997–2002), Warren Ellis's *Transmetropolitan* (1997–2002) and *Global Frequency* (2002–4), and even Frank Miller and Geoff Darrow's *Hard Boiled* (1990–92). Later on in *Masks of the Noh*, Mack explicitly lists William Gibson, one of the earliest cyberpunk writers, as one of his inspirations. Cyberpunk, whether American or Japanese, is typically near-future dystopian science fiction that thematizes humanity's descent into heavily technologized environments.

Kabuki is a highly recognizable character type of 1990s American comics. *Kabuki* is affiliated, however loosely, with the bad-girl comics of that decade and the exoticization of Japanese/Asian culture of the same period. The series, however, is far more informed by elements of Japanese culture, history, and language than similar series from that period. The first appearance of Kabuki was in July 1994 in *Razor/Shi Special*, released by the publisher London Night. This issue was a one-off crossover comic that primarily connected the two characters Razor and Shi, from the comic *Shi*, by William Tucci, that ran from 1994 to 1997 with later miniseries in the early 2000s and a reboot in 2020. Although *Kabuki* continued on with Caliber Comics, the guest appearance is telling. Both *Razor* and *Shi* were part of the 1990s onslaught of bad-girl comics. Their bad-girl characters are typically violent martial artist assassins who scoff at clothing. These nimbos (ninja bimbos) include "Psylocke (Marvel), Shi (Crusade), Avengelyne (Image), Razor (London Night) and Dawn (Sirius)."[6] Kabuki must be included in this list since there are several variant covers and guest renditions of Kabuki that tie in with this practice of sexualizing the main female character. Yet at the same time we rarely find moments of sexploitation or instances of the male gaze in the comic itself. *Fear the Reaper* does indulge in this practice, but *Kabuki* as a series outgrows this deplorable trend quickly.

After this initial brief story, the volume *Circle of Blood* begins, published by Caliber Comics in six issues in 1995. Most of *Circle of Blood* alternates between present-time Kabuki hunting Ryuichi Kai and past events revealing that General Kai was the husband of Tsukiko, a comfort woman who is also the mother of Ukiko. However, General Kai is the grandfather of Ukiko, not the father, because Ryuichi Kai raped and impregnated Tsukiko. After the crime, he carved the word "Kabuki" into Tsukiko's back. Ryuichi chooses this word due to General Kai's love of kabuki performances, performances in which Tsukiko participated. This introduces an anachronism. *Kabuki* is set in an unspecified future, although General Kai fought in World War II. However, women were banned from participating in kabuki performances by government decree in 1629.[7] General Kai is portrayed as a willful maverick who transgresses by having women perform, yet little more is made of this fact.

As present-time Kabuki murders her way through the Kai Syndicate, we learn through flashbacks that Ryuichi Kai attacked Ukiko at her mother's grave, carving "Kabuki" into her face and leaving her dead on her mother's grave. General Kai intervened and Ukiko was resuscitated, after having been dead for nine minutes. General Kai trained Ukiko to become Kabuki, the most fearsome assassin of the Noh. Kabuki manages to find Ryuichi Kai to kill him but fails. *Circle of Blood* ends as Kabuki, shot to pieces and bleeding out, staggers to her mother's grave and collapses, dying again in the same position as when she was nine. Tragedy repeats.

The *Dreams* volume consists of four disparate issues published by Caliber Comics and Image Comics in 1996, 1999, and 2002. Although its publication is scattered across several years, the story chronology overlaps with the ending of *Circle of Blood* and the first half restates the same events but focalizes them differently, and the illustration style is markedly different. Internally focalized through Kabuki as she is dying, the story we are presented with is more of Ukiko's past and her memories of her mother. The second half of *Dreams* remains hallucinatory but slowly moves the story forward; Kabuki is resuscitated again: "The heart beats. Grows louder. It pulls me back into my skin."[8] This concludes the *Dreams* collection, even as the *Kabuki* story line has continued elsewhere.

After the *Dreams* collection there is a split in the story line. One story line, *Masks of the Noh*, follows the other Noh agents looking for Kabuki, while the other story line, *Skin Deep*, stays with Kabuki and her escape from a nefarious organization called Control Corps. *Masks of the Noh* was published in four issues by Caliber Comics from 1996 to 1997. The issues shift perspectives between the different Noh agents and their search, each getting a little closer to finding Kabuki. In the end, Tigerlily finds Kabuki dying on her mother's grave, bringing us back to the end of *Circle of Blood*. Tigerlily is injured and collapses on Kabuki's mother's grave in the same position as Kabuki, while Kabuki is rushed to the hospital. Events repeat again. *Masks of the Noh* expands on the other Noh agents' stories, especially the relationship between Tigerlily and Scarab, and is largely disconnected from Kabuki's story, even though she remains a central plot element.

We revert to Kabuki's story line with *Skin Deep*, published in three issues by Caliber Comics in 1996 and 1997, meaning there is an overlap in publication with *Masks of the Noh*. *Skin Deep* reveals more about how Kabuki was saved as an adult

(Siamese were able to get her from her mother's grave, onto a helicopter, and to a hospital). Kabuki is now in an asylum, run by the Control Corps, a new organization that attempts to learn more about the Noh. Refusing to reveal anything about the Noh, Kabuki spends most of her time remembering her mother and her past, while also receiving notes from Akemi, another inmate. Akemi is a new and central character who at first is potentially a hallucination in Kabuki's mind but turns out to be an ally. Control Corps is revealed to have captured many former Noh agents due to their mental breakdowns. Interspersed with Kabuki's dreams and therapeutic discussions are scenes of the other Noh agents trying to find Kabuki and kill her before she reveals any secrets.

These events continue without interruption in *Metamorphosis*, published by Image Comics from 1997 to 2000. This volume essentially continues the story line from *Skin Deep*, with Kabuki ruminating on her identity. Akemi and Kabuki's relationship develops, and increasingly Kabuki comes to see herself as Ukiko again, rather than the Noh agent Kabuki. *Metamorphosis* concludes with the Noh agents breaking into the asylum as Ukiko escapes. Both *Skin Deep* and *Metamorphosis* take place in the restricted setting of the asylum, which means that the world feels less futuristic and is far more focused on the psychological aspects of Kabuki and her struggles with reality and identity. Although there are action and fight scenes in these two collections, there is a genre reframing to a far more character-centered drama.

In another story line split, the collection *Scarab: Lost in Translation* is parallel storywise with *Skin Deep* and *Metamorphosis* and expands on the growing relationship between Tigerlily and Scarab, focalized primarily through Scarab. *Scarab* was published by Image Comics from 1999 to 2001 and so overlaps with the publication of *Metamorphosis*, though there is little connection between the two stories. Kabuki makes minor appearances but is mostly irrelevant to the story, except for a crucial overlap that becomes the focus of an important analytic discussion I pursue in chapter 4. This collection is not illustrated by David Mack but by Rick Mays. Mays is an American comics artist who had previously worked for Marvel on the *Nomad* series (1992–94) and would go on to do work for Marvel, DC, and Image Comics with runs on *Robin*, *X-Men Unlimited*, and *Cyblade*. His visual style is in part inspired by seinen manga, adding to the Japanese influence and feel of *Scarab*. The story elaborates on the Noh TV series, but the world feels less futuristic than in the earliest *Kabuki* volumes.

The Alchemy concludes the *Kabuki* story line. It was published in nine issues by Marvel Comics from 2004 to 2007. There is little left of the SF action-thriller that *Kabuki* was when it started. Ukiko has escaped the asylum, locates a veterinarian, and gets help fleeing Japan. She takes a flight from Japan to the United States, encountering a comics writer-artist on the plane. While writing letters to Akemi, Ukiko finds herself, becomes pregnant, and overthrows the Noh by writing a tell-all comic with the help of the comic book writer-artist she met on the plane—a man named David Mack.

In relation to *Kabuki*'s position within a longer comics poetics, across its volumes *Kabuki* features a wide array of styles that shift to accommodate changing moods and story lines, but this is not the only comic to do so. While this is not the place for a history of comics, placing *Kabuki* in its cultural-historical context is helpful for understanding its style. The page layouts and drawing style in one book do not persist into the next; there is a change in style from *Fear the Reaper* to *The Alchemy* that goes beyond stylistic maturation. Overall, *Kabuki* exhibits a tendency to experiment with page layouts and graphic styles. Dreams, hallucinations, and near-death visions produce spatial arrangements in ways that explore the potentials of the "waffle iron" layout—the most regular of comics layouts, having panels of the same size on every page—and other page layouts.[9] Throughout the development of the series, Mack increasingly moves toward splash pages rather than gridded pages. Yet most of his splash pages retain a sense of spatial direction that is not divested from page grids. This spatial experimentation is a crucial part of both *Kabuki*'s expression and my analysis of the series.

One obvious inspiration that Mack has often acknowledged is Bill Sienkiewicz's style, especially in his and Frank Miller's *Elektra: Assassin*. Several of the panels and page layout ideas reverberate in *Kabuki*'s pages. Most of Sienkiewicz's work incorporates mixed-media elements, a strategy that Mack later followed. Dave McKean's work, such as *Violent Cases* (with Neil Gaiman, 1987) and *Arkham Asylum* (with Grant Morrison, 1989), is also prior to *Kabuki* and also informs Mack's style. A fellow traveler, Sam Kieth, especially his series *The Maxx* that was published one year before *Kabuki*, should be mentioned. Genre- and storywise, the two series are nothing alike (except for a superficial allegiance to superhero comics), but in terms of shifting styles and unconventional approaches to space and time, they are quite similar. Kieth also alternates graphic styles to accommodate the mood of the story and often switches styles even within a single issue. Changes of style within a single issue are not unusual and can be found in recent work by Matt Fraction and Chip Zdarsky's *Sex Criminals* (Image Comics, 2013–20). What matters is the way that style participates in the story and how spatial relations are part of this change in style, which goes beyond illustration and is also part of the page layout.

Kabuki thus stands as a typical comic book. David Mack's style negotiates page layouts within the confines of a rectangular page. Throughout his work, that page shape allows him to explore spatial form, as it pertains to both the classic grid and the splash page. This is something that every comics artist faces—how to best shape space to express their ideas. Spatial form is always part of how comics express stories.

Spatial Poetics

Space is Mack's calling card; it serves as the best pathway into his aesthetic style and a formalist analysis of *Kabuki*. In fact, I will argue that *Kabuki* expresses a primacy of the spatial. Most comics scholarship turns on either the primacy of the image, preferring the visual, or the primacy of stories, preferring the narrative. Mack is every bit as invested in visual storytelling as any other comics artist. However, when we emphasize the visual aspect of comics, we emphasize the image as the predominant signifier. While images certainly are important for comics, several comics theorists have complained that such overemphasis on the image cannot explain the dynamic nature of comics. Groensteen most strongly rejects basing comics theory on a fetishization of the image and instead embraces a spatio-topical system that integrates visual and discursive codes.[10] Karin Kukkonen's introduction to comics studies is less vocal about the distinction between the visual and the spatial yet quietly notes that comics "have images," not that they *are* images.[11] She continues to emphasize the relations of panels and compositions on the page over the specific visual codes of panels. Jan Baetens and Hugo Frey, in their book *The Graphic Novel*, also posit "juxtaposed images" as the crucial aspect of comics, rather than simply images.[12] In other words, space is the place where comics happen.

My argument for a spatial poetics also follows a classic argument in comics theory— Pierre Fresnault-Deruelle's point that space is the signifier in comics.[13] Fresnault-Deruelle argues that the page layout becomes a crucial structure for comics and their narratives, organizing both narrative events and reading flow. Although he never moves beyond the richness of the page, there is good reason to conceptualize page sequences, much as issues and collections are also spatial. Especially for a comics series such as *Kabuki*, where panels and page layouts return and repeat across collections, there is a need to understand the distance between such repetitions as important for narrative and mood. The comics assemblage is three-dimensional; not simply the two dimensions of the page (width and height) but the distance between panels, events, and recurring motifs and page layouts serves as an intensive marker of connection (depth). Whether this works as flashbacks, narrative emphasis, or some other function, this spatial aspect remains significant. Comics are not sculpture, so this third dimension exists as an aspect of the reading experience. Yet since such connections are narrative structures, they are not subjective-individual realizations but part of comics' spatial form.

Spatial form is not divested from comics' visual form but an attempt at understanding how visual elements are arranged spatially. Allied with Charles Hatfield's material theory of comics as a "nesting of spaces" navigable in "an architectonic way," spatial form conceives of comics as three-dimensional.[14] On the comics page we find the conventional two-dimensional space of height and width. Across the sequences of issues, collections, and so on, we find a three-dimensional space of connections in depth. These connections may be closer or farther apart, in parallel to how panels are arranged on the individual or splash page. My exploration of spatial form is thus an exploration of these spatially contingent connections that develop in three dimensions. In this way, spatial form suggests that different parts of the panel and page (and sequence) take up specific locations within the comics assemblage and that spatial location is pregnant with meaning.

1. *Kabuki: Circle of Blood*, act 2.

Space and spatial form are prominent ways in which Mack's visual expression and storytelling take form. Here are some typical examples. The opening pages of *Circle of Blood* immediately announce the complexity of space and how gridding is a part of such spatial complexity. The first page has six panels: three smaller, mostly white ones on the left side of the page, and three larger, mostly black ones on the right side of the page. A large amount of white space surrounds all the panels. But the panels do not directly connect; no narrative emerges sequentially across these six panels. The three left-side panels continue across the verso page as a television intro on the Noh channel. The three right-side panels continue on the recto page as seven panels—one with two panels side by side and two panels making up one image of a woman's face superimposed on a city landscape. While the Noh TV panels constitute a sustained action, the other panels function as mostly disjointed images of Tokyo. Time isn't evenly distributed across the sides of the pages. The left side of the Noh TV imagery probably takes about a few seconds of a zoom-in close-up. The right side of the Tokyo images takes however long it takes for the reader to read the captions and digest the images—there is no sense of an objective duration for these images. And these two distinct durations do not correlate—the Noh TV and Tokyo overview sequences have no direct temporal connection to each other.

Similarly, Mack's double splash pages often combine multiple events across different time lines into the same space. A typical example is in act 2 of *Circle of Blood*. Once again, the spatial form of the double spread is the main attraction in terms of both narrative and temporal expression. Ice, one of the Noh agents, is introduced in a double splash page. Ice appears twice in the same panel, once hanging off the wall and once standing over grotesque ape-men. The inserted panels give a highly cursory suggestion of the unfolding event, while the main panel provides the beginning and end of the event. Time is presented as still moments; little suggestion of movement is evident, and the effect is almost stroboscopelike. Brief flashes of images combine into a larger whole—Ice attacks the ape-men and kills them.

Putting forth spatial poetics as a way of understanding comics is not meant to override other comics theories or to somehow falsify them. It is rather to provide a framework that allows these different theories to come into contact with each other and coexist peacefully. Poetics is the larger study of aesthetic forms, and so spatial poetics emphasizes the spatial aspects of comics' aesthetic forms. Spatial poetics is here understood as the way spatial configurations of line, panel, page, and other visual elements produce a variety of aesthetic effects. With everything from page layout to repeating panels and motifs, sequential series contribute to the expressive form of a comic.

Spatial poetics is useful because visual design is spatial and narrative theories are also spatial in the way that comics must necessarily convert space to time and action. Spatial poetics agrees with, for instance, Neil Cohn's visualist-sequential approach—that panels are neither arbitrary signs nor a closed lexicon.[15] In the same vein, spatial poetics agrees with Mikkonen's narratological argument that it is not the gutter that produces meaning in comics but the relation between panels—an argument also made by Groensteen.[16] What has been largely left out, however, has been the spatial form of these panel relations.

Arguing for spatial form in comics is hardly new. The most elaborate work done in terms of space and comics is Groensteen's spatio-topological system, outlined in *The System of Comics* and *Comics and Narration*. Groensteen's premise is straightforward and spatial. He defines comics, as we have seen, in terms of *iconic solidarity*; panels and their internal elements, like character figures, speech balloons, and captions, are placed in spatial relation to external elements, such as other panels, pages, series, and so on.[17] Comics emerge from these various relations either as linear relations (termed "restricted arthrology"), such as panel to panel or page to page, or as translinear relations ("general arthrology"), such as series to series, panels repeated across different volumes, page to genre, or any other form of relation.

In this view, comics are networks; meaning, signification, and experience arise from these network relations. As Bukatman puts it, a comic exists as "a network that encompasses the relation of panel-to-panel, panel-to-page, story-to-story, story-to-series, series-to-series, and series-to-genre."[18] Conceiving of comics as networks is helpful, in particular due to their sequential and serial nature, and it also avoids placing too much emphasis on the space between panels—the infamous gutter that Scott McCloud has made a central element of comics. The gutter produces the comics experience through the reader's operation of closure that turns "a *jagged, staccato rhythm* of *unconnected moments*" into "a *continuous, unified reality*."[19] In McCloud's view, no gutter means no comics. Groensteen decries McCloud's emphasis on the space between images, since "all the voids probably don't have the same value."[20] Furthermore, making comics revolve around what is not there deemphasizes what *is* there. I have never met a comics reader excited about what the artist did not draw. While McCloud's notion of the invisible art (as he calls comics) is well put, we need to get our minds out of the gutter and on the same page: the page is what organizes the experience of comics. That page is necessarily a spatial arrangement, whether there are gutters or not. The position of any visual element on the panel, page, and series participates in the production of sense and meaning, as with Ice's different placements discussed above. Spatial arrangements generate dynamic effects through their relations; spatial arrangements are what make comics come alive for readers.

One of the most intriguing arguments for comics as spatial relations unfortunately remains mostly unpublished. Rikke Platz Cortsen's dissertation, "Comics as Assemblage: How Spatio-Temporality in Comics Is Constructed" (2012), introduces the idea of assemblage as an alternative to the network. Drawing on Manuel DeLanda's work on the Deleuzian assemblage, Cortsen argues for a dynamic framework to explain comics' capacity to realize a wide variety of connections and disconnections.[21] Cortsen's connections and disconnections are essentially Groensteen's relations—how panel elements, panels, pages, and more combine to produce an experiential field. The main advantage of assemblage over network is the productive element of components in an assemblage. Whereas a network mainly works through its connections, an assemblage, as DeLanda has shown, works both through its individual components and through the integration of these same components. We can think of this in relation to Groensteen's paradox of panels being both separate and coexisting. A panel signifies on its own, *and* it signifies in relation to the rest of the comics assemblage. This is not to overstate the difference between network and assemblage, only to clarify my preferred terminology.

Comics' spatial poetics fits within a larger discussion of spatial form. Spatial form was first introduced in literary studies as a way of understanding how modernist writings disrupted regular continuities (in language) with disjunctive syntactic arrangements. This argument was made by Joseph Frank in the essay "Spatial Form in Modern Literature," originally published in 1945. In it, Frank argues that modernist writers (Pound, Proust, Joyce, and especially Djuna Barnes) "intend their readers to apprehend their work spatially, in a moment in time, rather than as a sequence."[22] Of course, this sounds like the exact opposite of what comics scholarship thinks of how time and space are expressed. The consensus is that apprehending the comic book spatially *is* the temporal sequence. And yet, no comics scholar would feel that the situation is that straightforward—there is no consensus on how or in what way time is expressed through panels, either internally in the individual panel or through panel transitions.

W. J. T. Mitchell cuts through a lot of the noise, even though he is not addressing comics directly: "the experience of simultaneity or discontinuity is simply based in different kinds of spatial images from those involved in continuous, sequential experiences of time."[23] For Mitchell, for Groensteen, for Cortsen, and for me, the way these spatial forms make experience possible is what matters. These spatial forms are what constitute a spatial poetics.

Spatial poetics is therefore a concern with how comics work. I am less interested in interpretative questions of what comics mean and instead curious about the formal features and components that make comics signify. In this way, spatial poetics is not the same as a poetics of space (such as Gaston Bachelard's) but may well borrow from it. As readers of comics, we do inhabit a world of space, and we inhabit that world in particular ways. Spatial poetics is also different from the spatial turn that has been making the rounds in the humanities recently. I am concerned with spatial layouts, not the spaces presented in them.

The main argument for a spatial poetics is that space must be understood as a relational arrangement, not as a static category. Mitchell draws on Leibniz's idea of space as an order of coexistent data because, in such a conception, space is "both relational and kinematic, allowing for multiple orders of data in complex relationships."[24] To say that space is kinematic is not to suggest that comics are subordinate to cinema but to emphasize that there is by necessity a sense of movement generated through spatial assemblage. As Frank points out, experiences form new wholes.[25] A comics panel exists as the locus of narrative and affective tensions. Importantly, this locus is never static but dynamic; the locus constantly morphs into new relations, attaching to new meanings, significations, and expressions. The comics panel is always already part of a larger spatial assemblage.

Comics are spaces of possibilities with what DeLanda terms, after Deleuze, extensive and intensive properties. Extensive properties can be divided without change; a page can be cut in half and we would have two halves of a page. Intensive properties "*cannot be divided without involving a change in kind*."[26] A comics page whose layout is changed (to have fewer or more panels, for example) would not generate the same reading experience. Although comics clearly have extensive properties, the reading experience comes from the intensive properties of the page layout, the panel components, the panel and page interaction, the page interaction with the other pages, the series, the genre, and so on. The spatial poetics of comics is a matter of the comics' "*intensive space*."[27] A changed page layout presents different reading experiences. I am taking DeLanda's ideas in a direction that he did not anticipate. I do so by extending Cortsen's argument about comics as assemblage and the larger field of comics scholarship that acknowledges the spatial dynamic inherent in the medium. In this manner, spatial relations become paramount for understanding the comics assemblage.

The comics assemblage that I am interested in here consists of four different spatial forms: rhymes, choreographies, perspectives, and rhythms. The first chapter deals with spatial rhymes. Spatial rhymes are nontemporal linkages of motifs across panels, pages, and collections. These linkages work to intensify mood through graphic similarities and contrasts. One of *Kabuki*'s main features is the repetition and variation of panels and panel elements that establish consonance across the different collections and reinforce thematic concerns. Exploring the potentials of spatial rhymes contributes to a better understanding of internal and external page relations through the repetition and variation of panel elements. This provides a more granular and more exact terminology for analyzing comics' spatial relations. These spatial relations may be suggestive of reading flow (which direction should readers follow) as well as the mood of the story.

Chapter 2 examines the spatial choreography of time. Conventionally, this discussion focuses on the sequence of panels, which is also a key concern for *Kabuki*. There are two other devices at work in *Kabuki*, however. One is lack of movement, almost a sense of stillness in some panels. The other is the use of mixed-media styles to suggest a layering of multiple temporalities simultaneously on the same panel or page. This idea of a spatial choreography is a contribution to the study of how time is expressed in comics. Time can overlap in comics; several events that are disconnected may be layered (what I will call folded) on the same page. Such folding of time is one way in which comics exhibit a highly flexible expression of time that cannot be captured through a focus on sequence.

Perspective is the focus of the third chapter, understood in its broadest sense of narration, focalization, and spatial positioning. These three terms speak to the different positionings of narrational instances, and while this may seem less overtly spatial, *Kabuki* expresses these different instances spatially through various graphic style shifts, as well as panel and page composition and design. Perspectives, both literal and narrative, are knotted together. This chapter therefore contributes to issues of focalization and spatial perspective, an important aspect of comics storytelling due to its visual nature, an issue touched on by Mieke Bal.[28] Who sees versus who speaks is a very different question in comics than it is in literature, and perspective is bound up with that question.

The topic of rhythms concludes the main portion of this study, with chapter 4 analyzing sequential patterns across panels, pages, and collections. While sequence connects with spatial form, chapter 4 focuses on the rhythms that form from panel sizes and repetition. In this way, my analysis expands on the narrative vocabulary of rhythms that are mostly concerned with purely temporal-durational concerns.[29] This chapter therefore loops back to the first to discuss the temporal linkages of repeated panels and motifs that are so prevalent in *Kabuki*. Finally, rhythms of the frame are discussed as instances of metalepses—the paradoxical frame-breaking of narrative levels between our real world and the fictional world of *Kabuki* in the encounter of Kabuki and David Mack. This frame-breaking is spatial as much as it is narrative in *Kabuki*, and so my discussion expands on Gérard Genette's classic discussion of metalepsis.[30] Once these narrative levels have been broken, the story of Kabuki concludes, as does this study.

1
Spatial Rhymes

Linkages and Refrains

One of the ways *Kabuki* privileges space is through its use of recurring panels and motifs within and across collections. Recurring panels are not simply used as flashbacks or flashforwards but also add atmosphere to the story. For this reason, these recurring panels do not obey a narrative logic but instead follow the logic of a rhyme. Rhyme is thus an idea of correspondence, a similarity between panels, panel elements, or page structures. How that correspondence is established may differ—it can be either repetition or resemblance. *Kabuki* tends toward both repetition and resemblance; many panels are repeated exactly, and there are several graphic motifs that continue across pages.

For some reason, rhymes have not been investigated much in comics studies. Neil Cohn briefly brings up the idea of rhyming but does not expand on it, only comparing it to a thematic leitmotif.[1] Pierre Fresnault-Deruelle posits rhymes as a formal element that exceeds the individual page and so modulates narrative cohesion.[2] Thierry Groensteen also briefly mentions rhymes in *The System of Comics*, where he identifies rhyming with citational practice as a distant repetition within the same work (though not necessarily the same issue). Distant repetition suggests that the repeated panel must not be too close to the first occurrence of the panel. When repetition occurs closely together, Groensteen instead terms it an insistence—an emphasis of the panel's event. It is unclear to me why distant repetition is rhyme but close repetition is insistence (and not rhyme).[3] Chris Gavaler follows Groensteen's conception of rhyme but associates it only with braiding, rather than expanding the notion as I do here.[4]

We can say that rhymes suggest thematic and narrative emphasis, while also opening up the possibility for connections and associations across pages. Rhymes have the potential for being a crucial component of the comics assemblage, a connector that impacts the felt proximity of the rhyme elements. That is to say, a rhyme pattern brings its elements closer together (intensively), even if they are otherwise far apart (extensively). This is one way in which rhymes are a matter of space—they alter the spatial relations between elements across pages. The other rhyme pattern comprises the ways in which the page layout may itself produce associations; the location on the page of the rhyme motif may in itself produce emphasis.

As Derek Attridge defines rhyme in his discussion of poetry, rhyme is a patterning effect and a structural device that emerges from "the repetition of the stressed vowel of a word and any sounds that follow it, combined with a difference in the consonant immediately preceding it."[5] Although word rhymes certainly exist in comics (and do in *Kabuki* in the form of song lyrics and *Alice in Wonderland* quotations), that is not my interest here. Instead, I take Attridge's larger point about patterns, structural devices, and repetition to be applicable to graphic motifs, panels, and page layouts. That is to say, poetry (and the study of poetry) provides helpful analytic insight and terminological accuracy in relation to repeated panels and page structures.

Rhyme patterns are *spatial* even more so than they are *visual*. This is not to deny that comics are a predominantly visual medium but to emphasize that the comics assemblage follows a spatial logic. In fact, the usefulness of rhyme is as a structural device that produces connections and emphasis simultaneously. In this conception, rhymes become ways of arranging space in meaningful ways. While in written poetry, rhyme schemes form based on sound patterns, in comics rhymes are spatial patterns—arrangements of panels and motifs in spatially intensive ways. Also, by following a broader definition of rhyme, such as Attridge's, rhyme is also liberated from having to be an exact reproduction. Just as words rhyme with others words, so motifs may rhyme with other motifs. We can consider multiple different cases as instances of rhymes in comics—similar but not identical images, panel compositions, page layouts, and so forth.

Rhymes are thus the first major foray into spatial poetics in this book because spatial relations are imbued with significance through their position rather than their content. This argument follows from Groensteen's argument for iconic solidarity as the cornerstone of comics—rhymes are instances of solidarity expressed spatially. Rhymes may manifest through resemblance and through location, either on the page or across pages; in both cases it is their spatial solidarity that produces the rhyming pattern. The rhyming pattern produces different relations than the sequential pattern of one panel after another.

Groensteen perceptively insists that no repeated panel can ever be the same, since it is necessarily different because it does not occupy the same space. Comics' relational aesthetics depend on positioning for their expression and so any otherwise identical panel positioned differently also generates a different experience. This is a variation of what I distinguished as extensive versus intensive; any change in the assemblage registers as a change in experience. This is also why Groensteen's distinction between citation and insistence is so peculiar. Any repeated panel is both citation and insistence. Furthermore, Groensteen really discusses textual memory when he uses

the term "citational." Although intertextual citations occur, repeated panels function as a narrative memory to establish certain events as more important than others.

However, Groensteen never really broaches the most interesting aspect of spatial rhymes—the rhyming of similar motifs that connect and intensify important aspects of the story line. For Groensteen, through the sequence and the network run two systems: the narrative, which obeys a syntagmatic logic, and the symbolic, which obeys an associative logic.[6] The associative logic is termed "braiding" and weaves significance together across distant panels, bringing them into synchronic and diachronic co-presence.[7] Braiding is left vague by Groensteen, since it can take so many forms. Rhyme can be one aspect of braiding, although it is not limited to it. To gain some terminological clarity, I distinguish between *linkage*, which is any kind of rhyming motif, and *refrain*, which is a repeating function. I open up Groensteen's idea by freeing them from being only citational or insistent, only distant or contiguous. In this way, I do not reject Groensteen's concept of rhyme or braiding but seek to develop his ideas further by bringing in more concepts to build a stronger vocabulary.

For an example of how rhyming works in *Kabuki*, consider page 84 in *Skin Deep*, part 3: "Paper Tiger." It is a splash page presenting Tigerlily. The top third of the page is a watercolor tiger, half in black and white, the other half in color with deep red blood drops as background on an otherwise white page. There are no panels on this page, although there are three different elements that divide the page. The captions that run across the page tie it together with narrative information that anchors the images.

There are no directly repeated panels or motifs here, but the

2. *Kabuki: Skin Deep*, 84.

page is rich in correspondences. First, the tiger, stork, and dog are all instances of linkages that produce a spatial form from top to bottom, guiding the eye through similar animal motifs. The tiger is the main motif due to its sheer size, and the stork and dog are rhymes that assist the flow of reading but also produce linkage through the animal motifs, suggesting that the end of the tiger (its tail becomes the stork) brings the child, which leads to the dog. There is a graphic correspondence between tiger, stork, and dog in that they are all animals.

The animals are all visual elements on the page; the rhyme that emerges from these visual elements is particular space produced from the layout relations across the page. This intensive space produces the tiger-stork-dog movement, which encapsulates and circumscribes the family; one within the other, they are connected and exist because of each other. This rhyme adds mood to the page and links the various graphic elements in a way that goes beyond the narrative. Because the animal rhyme guides the reading flow, there is also a shift away from the Noh and toward a higher degree of normality, something also expressed in the shift of graphic style.

A different rhyme emerges in the preceding and following pages as a part of the animal motif. Part 3 of *Skin Deep* opens with a double splash page that has an origami tiger, which unfolds to turn into a drawn tiger that turns into a spiral movement of other origami animals (bird, elephant, pig, horse, etc.) that form a rhyme across these two pages. The central motif is the back of a woman with the Noh dragon tattoo—a unifying marker of all the Noh agents. The graphic matches identify the woman as Tigerlily, intensifying the relations across the pages. The tiger motif rhymes across pages 82, 83, and 84, creating a graphic motif that links the pages together and returns as a contrast on the double splash page (86) as a small, stuffed tiger. There is another rhyme on pages 83 and 85: Tigerlily's back and tattoo in an identical pose and almost identical position on the page. This rhyme between tiger and dragon suggests a tension between animals and belonging to the Noh.

For Tigerlily this tension is between the Noh agents' deadly work and the caring work of the family, with the rhyme contrast expressed through the shift in graphic style between the actual tiger and the stuffed tiger. By rhyming with the tiger across the Tigerlily story line and the Kabuki-Akemi story line, the tension of Tigerlily is brought into contact with the tension of the Kabuki-Akemi story line. This is how a spatial rhyme may link different elements together, thus creating a coherent whole that remains nontemporal and non-narrative. The spatial rhymes of similar graphic motifs generate a complementary flow that adds mood and coherence to the pages. *Skin Deep* follows Kabuki while she is in a mental hospital, and much of her experience is jumbled and fragmented. While the narrative does not break down, neither does the story follow straightforwardly from the plot. The spatial flow of rhyming motifs makes *Kabuki*'s jumbled narrative structure easier to follow. Spatial flow also intensifies relations between characters, in this case Tigerlily and Kabuki, both of whom desire to leave the Noh.

Rhymes, then, turn out to be important structuring devices for story coherence, characterization, and thematic unity. For this reason, rhymes can exist in many different forms not restricted to repeated panels. While I would hesitate to say that catchphrases such as Ben Grimm's "It's clobberin' time" in *Fantastic Four* constitute rhymes, I would argue that Flash Thompson's recurring use of "Hail Mary" in Rick Remender's *Venom* (2015) would be an instance of a rhyme. Thompson's "Hail Mary" produces connections across the story by bringing tense, last-ditch efforts into contact with each other. If the phrase had been used repeatedly, or for every fight sequence, the instance would be closer to Grimm's "clobberin' time" catchphrase, which fits more within narrative and character expectations and does not structure the comics in any particular manner.

Not solely the province of a few rare comics, rhymes are found in much of the medium. In Sarah Vaughn and Jonathan Luna's *Alex + Ada* (2013–15), the first collection employs rhymes extensively to suggest the sameness of Alex's life, through the repeated panel layouts with minimal changes (pages 9–12). *Alex + Ada* also produces moments of protracted awkwardness, where repeated panels expand duration embarrassingly (57–58). Fábio Moon and Gabriel Bá's *Daytripper* (2010) uses a compositional rhyme to express the sadness of a lost relationship (61, 70, 71). The same panel composition repeats across the bottom and top of the three pages, the open door becomes a closed door that becomes a painting, with the rectangular shape in the same place and Brás's body in the same position, first sitting then standing in two of the panels. These examples are chosen somewhat arbitrarily to point out that rhyming is not restricted to any particular form, genre, or mode of comics.

Linkages

More than a stand-alone function, spatial rhymes can also bring coherence across a whole issue and link events more intensely to their narrative unfolding. "Scene IV: Through the Looking Glass" is the last chapter in *Fear the Reaper* and also works as a backstory for Kabuki's mother, Tsukiko, itself one of the most important aspects of the *Kabuki* series. Scene IV runs across thirteen pages (41–53) in volume 1 of *Kabuki Omnibus* and is a prime instance of spatial rhymes that move beyond graphic motifs to also utilize page locations as a means of producing linkage. There is no dialogue in the chapter, only Kabuki's narration through captions that run across the pages. Scene IV introduces a circle shape that connects events across time, place, and characters. In this way, the circle shape produces coherence that intensifies the narrative connections. As I trace below, the circle shape functions as linkage; it produces mood and emotional anchorage that intensify the narrative experience.

The first page (41), which is also the title page, has Kabuki in shadows, holding her mask to her face; her mask has been prominently featured throughout *Fear the Reaper* and has become an identifying feature of Kabuki. Deep shadows hide her eyes, and the background is entirely black, with her hands, arms, and mask in white. The next page is again a splash page of a starlit sky with the moon, the sun, and another sphere, which has a distorted reflection of Kabuki's mask and hands. The sun is in the upper-right corner, mostly outside of the panel, with the sphere dominating the page, and the moon in the center of the lower third of the page. Pinprick stars dot the sky. There is no narrative connection to the previous page; this is not an event that takes place as such but instead a dream or reverie.

Not only is the shift from page 41 to 42 purely associative instead of narrative, there is also no real-world physics or logics to the image. Instead, the page has dreamily transposed everyday life onto a new register. The juxtaposition of sun, sphere, and moon does not suggest narrative progression, nor is it an associative braiding, since the graphic elements are near each other, not distant. Instead, it is a spatial rhyme of repeating circular motifs. That is to say, the three circular elements become linked with each other due to proximity on the same page and their graphic expression. This association becomes a rhyme pattern for the rest of the chapter (and beyond).

The depth of significance of the sphere and of the circular spatial rhyme becomes apparent on the very next page. Page 43 is yet another full-page layout, with Kabuki standing in front of a massive grave. The burial vault is above ground, with a monolithic column monument and a spherical urn on top of the vault. This is Kabuki's mother's grave, which becomes a recurring motif throughout the rest of the series. Within scene IV the spatial rhyme is the urn that is now associated with the sphere from the preceding page. This page does not have any other circular graphic elements, but there is now a cluster of linkages of circular graphic motifs: moon, sun, sphere/urn, and Kabuki's mother.

The next two pages develop the rhyme, with a moon and blood drops carrying the same graphic motif (and the blood drops echoing the blood drops on page 16, the opening page of *Fear the Reaper*). The spatial relations of the moon and the blood drop are reinforced by being in the same location on different pages; if the second page were superimposed on the first, the moon and the blood drop would be in the same position. In this way, the page layout reinforces their spatial connections.

Page 46 reintroduces the sun, in a spatial match of the earlier blood drop's position and the moon in the same place. The sun and moon hover over a field with a taloned bird of prey. There is a shift in narration, away from the dream-like first page to a more clearly historical-biographical narration that still belongs to Kabuki but follows a linear chronology and is no longer within an oneiric register. It should be noted that the sun has been present earlier (on pages 32, 33, and 40) as the graphic design of Kabuki's costume, and circles have also been recurring graphic elements, in everything from the scope of a rifle to the graphic design of the Circle of the Noh. This is the moment when the circular graphic motifs take on a resonant aspect and begin to work on a deeper level.

The spatial rhymes intensify on page 47, which has a regular four-by-two grid design. The first panel mirrors the talons of the bird with a sickle across the sun. We see the face of Kabuki's mother in the rest of the seven panels, first in a medium close-up that reveals she is the one holding the sickle. As the panels progressively move closer to her face, it is lost in shadow on her right side—a motif that foreshadows Kabuki's disfigured face, although this is unknown to the reader at this point. The panels shift closer to her eyes, then her left eyeball, which reflects a person in a way that recalls Kabuki's distorted reflection in the sphere on page 42. The final panel shifts and has the talon in the space as the first panel, with Kabuki's mother's face taking the place of the sun and sickle. The linkage grows larger, including sun, moon, urn, Kabuki's mother, and even her eye—in other words, what she has seen and experienced. The talon produces its own rhyme of first and last panel and sets up the threat of the Japanese soldiers who enslave the Ainu women as "comfort women"—a euphemism for sex slaves.

The idea of linkage here shows us how tightly interwoven the panels are through their graphic expression. The panels reinforce each other and produce an effect that goes beyond the different panel transitions that Scott McCloud argues for and is better captured by Groensteen's iconic solidarity.[8] Linkage, however, is a purely graphic aspect that emphasizes mood, not narration or narrative structure. Linkage becomes an assemblage alongside the linear sequence that produces narrative action and the nonlinear braiding that produces large-scale coherence and association.[9] Sequence and braiding are primarily *differential* in that each panel necessarily presents some degree of variation. Linkage, however, is primarily *iterative* in that each panel necessarily presents some degree of repetition.

It is this iterative arrangement that links sun, moon, urn, mother, Kabuki, and later Japan and Kabuki's father. A jug on page 48 introduces a rhyme pattern with the urn, its rounded shape reminiscent of the sphere. As the jug breaks, its shards evoke the pattern of the islands that make up Japan, a circle emphasizing Hokkaido as the land of the Ainu, a people oppressed by the Japanese. The following panel, on page 49, links both jug and Japan with a flock of birds in the shape of the islands/shards and the sun as repeating the graphic motif of the circle around Hokkaido. These are rhymes that maintain the shape but not the resemblance: shards to Japanese islands to flock of birds. The lower four panels of page 49 maintain the circle shape of the sun, the half rhyme of the sickle, and a shift to the moon. The moon shape helps the shift to the next page, where the moon is linked to the general's bald, round head. Page 51 is another full page of Kabuki's mother with the general inserted as a blazing sun on the black silhouette of Kabuki's mother, a graphic element that repeats on page 52, with the sun and the moon on opposite sides of the full page turned smaller panel, and the circle shape maintained as well in the shape of the fan.

Everything culminates in the final page of scene IV and the *Fear the Reaper* story in a return to Kabuki in shadows. This repeating page now has Kabuki looking up at us, her eyes and teardrop visible and the moon present behind her. The linear sequence is broken in the shift from past recollection to present moment. A host of linkages can be seen to enrich this last page. Kabuki's mask now has a direct association with her mother, the stylized tear on the mask connects to the mother crying on the previous page due to her grief. The moon in the background similarly recalls the mother's presence as the object of mourning. Yet that moon also maintains spatial rhymes of not just the moon but the sun (who is the father), the urn of the mother's death, the shards of the broken jug that evoke Japan and the breaking of the Ainu culture (enslaved to Japanese warlords), the sickle of peaceful farmers that becomes Kabuki's preferred weapon.

Linkage, then, allows us to recognize the associative richness of this final page that is graphically quite minimalist. The end of the rhyme sequence, however, finds all the previous linkages carried into this page, and we see the many rhyming motifs culminating in the page layout. This is another instance of how space intensifies the narrative, underlined by the fact that the moon drawing is literally the same drawing repeated across six separate pages. Clearly this repetition goes beyond the ease of reproduction to insist that this repeating element is significant in itself. The same goes for the full page of Kabuki's mother with the father inserted in a blazing sun. This page is literally copied as a panel on the next page. Repetition is important in *Fear the Reaper* and the *Kabuki* series as a whole, and linkage is what connects these repeating elements.

In the case of *Fear the Reaper*, linkage is overdetermined in that this is the origin story for Kabuki. For that reason, many different story and world elements must be clarified and brought into contact with each other. That does not mean, however, that linkage is restricted to *Fear the Reaper* or that it is even particularly dominant here as opposed to the rest of the *Kabuki* series. Already in *Circle of Blood*, spatial rhymes emerge to produce linkage back to *Fear the Reaper*. In act 1, Kabuki's mother is present only as eyes and mouth on a white background. This image runs through several pages (73–75) to establish her presence.

On pages 86 and 87 this graphic expression returns in seven of the two-by-two panel breakdowns. The story explains how Ryuichi Kai, the son of the general, has raped and disfigured Tsukiko by cutting out her eyes. In the top panel, Tsukiko's face is in the upper center of the panel, with tree branches on either side of her stylized face and the sun from *Fear the Reaper* in the bottom center. Across the next five panels, the sun turns into a fetus and then a baby, while the tree branches drop their leaves and become skeletal hands. The final panel that ends the sequence is a rhyme with the final page of *Fear the Reaper*. Kabuki holds her mask, the moon in the top corner. A new element is the urn from Tsukiko's grave; it rhymes with the urn from page 42 of *Fear the Reaper*, only it is turned 90 degrees. All the linked associations of *Fear the Reaper* are thus present in this final panel in another strong example of linkage, even across separate books.

Linkages are a crucial component of *Kabuki*'s assemblage and a major formal device for connecting elements across series and collections. Linkages' formal function produces an ordering in addition to the fundamental panel-strip-page. While linkage is clearly similar to Groensteen's braiding, it should also be clear that there is an important difference: linkages are not narrative sequences. Linkages are instead connections that add mood and atmosphere.

Refrains

There is a repetition that flows across all of *Kabuki*: the grave of Tsukiko, Kabuki's mother. The repetition exists both on a narrative level, where the reader is introduced to the grave in *Fear the Reaper* as part of Kabuki's reverie, and then later in *Circle of Blood* as a recurring motif, both the first time that Kabuki (almost) dies as a young girl at Kai's hand and when she is (almost) killed again by Kai when she is a Noh agent. In the narrative, Kabuki's double death and rebirth is a plot motif that also repeats—Tsukiko's death as that which gives birth to Kabuki. On the level of rhyme, the grave returns far more often than any other motif and takes on a host of associations of memory, dream, hallucination, and mourning. At least one panel of Tsukiko's grave is present in all the *Kabuki* collections, except *The Alchemy*. The grave is even present in the first *Kabuki* spin-off, *Masks of the Noh*.

The grave's presence varies depending on the collection and tends to show up in clusters. The grave is present once in *Fear the Reaper* (page 43), eleven times in *Circle of Blood* (89, 90, 93, 159, 184, 185, 209, 220, 245, 246, 247), seven in *Dreams* (262, 263,

264, 265, 267, 275, 276), twice in the spin-off *Masks of the Noh* (62, 63), three times in *Skin Deep* (21, 22, 23), and three times in *Metamorphosis* (124, 125, 296). There is a certain rhythm to the grave's return, which is why I list the instances here. I also wish to signal the repetition of this singular panel, for it is almost always exactly the same panel and the same angle of presentation. More than iteration, the grave is a matter of direct repetition, which is also known as a refrain.

Let us explore the idea of the refrain a little more. In poetry and verse, a refrain is a line that repeats at regular or irregular intervals. Often placed at the end of a stanza, the refrain is a clear instance of a rhyme scheme. As a spatial rhyme, the refrain draws together aspects of the story across the collections into an expressive unity, one that is best understood as mood rather than an explicit narrative element. The mood of *Kabuki* is established through this constant evocation of Kabuki's mother's grave. Because of the visual resemblance, this panel becomes a refrain—the panel is a clear repetition, even with minor variations in later collections. Preserving the intensive dimension of the comics assemblage, the refrain connects elements that are otherwise far apart and brings them into intensive relations. Events, compositions, motifs—all are part of what produces narrative coherence by connecting and contracting space. This is part of the refrain's spatial nature; elements that are far apart are brought into proximity, both on the level of narrative and on the level of mood.

Refrain as a repetition that generates mood also questions Shlomith Rimmon-Kenan's distinction of constructive versus destructive repetition, where "constructive repetition emphasizes difference, destructive repetition emphasizes sameness (i.e., to repeat successfully is not to repeat)."[10] The grave emphasizes sameness as a unifying element across the collections. At the same time, the grave is generative of a certain mood of mourning, which suggests that the repetition of the refrain is constructive, that is, it produces the mood of mourning. To be fair, Rimmon-Kenan points to this constructive-destructive binary as a paradox. It would be better, perhaps, to emphasize that the refrain may repeat (as it does) but that it is also open—it produces linkage across its patterns.

An open repetition that produces linkage across its patterns brings up the issue of repetition versus difference. When the patterns change, evolve, and transform, so do the linkage and the repetition. The refrain points to the difference of the repetition—a difference that emerges in the way patterns connect and shift. The same image, the same panel, takes on different meanings as its relations to the surrounding panels change (and repeat). The transformation of the refrain, or the changing relationship between Kabuki and her mother and father, suggests transformations in the entire arc of the *Kabuki* series.

The repetition of the refrain across different story lines, as well as page and panel constructions, links certain moments and events within the *Kabuki* series. The grave remains the most consistent graphic refrain across the series and so constantly makes grief something that comes back, despite the current narrative unfolding within which the refrain occurs. The grave brings us back to a narrative event that is in itself repeated several times across Kabuki's life. The grave makes a monument out of the rape and subsequent death of Tsukiko. These are the events from which Ukiko/Kabuki follows. As a child Ukiko/Kabuki is attacked by her father and almost dies on her mother's grave. This event repeats when Kabuki is a Noh agent and attempts to murder her father, fails, and is left to die on her mother's grave (again). This refrain—mother–child daughter–adult daughter—generates consistency and coherence in all the *Kabuki* collections. These collections are all gathered into a familiar territory of events repeating themselves through a return to the grave. The collections are made into one narrative space through the intensive aspect of the refrain.

The recurrence of the mother, not just through the grave panel but as a graphic motif in many different locations, furthers this refrain as a resonance that echoes throughout all of Kabuki's life. For instance, the face of Tsukiko as a kabuki performer, with the traditional all-white visage having only the eyes and mouth as visible features, framed by black hair pinned back, is also an image that returns often and in many places, typically as background, as on pages 114 and 119 of *Metamorphosis*. This version of Tsukiko's face is the one established on page 73 of *Circle of Blood* and resonates from there across the collections, in a manner similar to the grave panel.

Always in the background, the same sad face mourns for her daughter, expressed through the tear that Kabuki integrates as part of her mask. This suggests an aspect of the page layout that I have not discussed so far—the use of foreground-background relations. While the comics page often uses perspectival techniques to suggest a three-dimensional space in its two dimensions, sometimes space is layered in a nonperspectival, nonrealist manner. For this sequence in *Kabuki*, the background does not provide a depth impression but instead evokes a mood—Kabuki's mother is always present for Kabuki. This may be viewed in two ways. First, it may be an objective instance of thematic reinforcement—what Cohn has termed a leitmotif. Second, it may be subjective access to Kabuki's thoughts and feelings wherein her mother is always present.

Whichever way we choose to understand this foreground-background relation, it becomes another way for space to produce relations both on the individual page and across pages. The mood of the individual page is saturated by the background image, which is at the same time related to the repetition of the background image as a refrain cutting across several pages and collections. This background refrain links all the different pages together in the same mood through its repetition.

These brief examples are only meant to gesture toward the general complexity of the return in *Kabuki* and to suggest that the refrain adds a high degree of thematic unity for *Kabuki* as a series. The series becomes a work of mourning, the process of grief and loss being an emotional core that incessantly comes back. Such a work of mourning is of course also quite literal on a biographical level. The entire *Kabuki* series is dedicated to David Mack's mother, and Mack has often stated in interviews and essays that he started *Kabuki* while his mother was dying. I do not want to pursue a biographical trauma reading here (although I believe such a reading is possible). I simply want to underline the ways in which the work of mourning is expressed "piecemeal," in "fits and starts rather than in a continuous, uninterrupted manner."[11] The refrain and the discontinuous nature of *Kabuki* are expressive of such a work of mourning.

More than anything, the refrain takes on a particular function within the comics assemblage, as it demarcates a particular string of connections across the assemblage. For the comics assemblage, this begins with the panel, and this observation is orthodox. The panel consists of a moment of time. A moment is a vague, flexible duration of time that may be of any length: a split second or an eternity. Whatever forces are within the panel are what make up the moment. The moment may well be expressed across several panels, and the moment is not restricted to only one panel but more accurately to the emergence of a movement, a slice of duration however long. A duration may certainly also unfold within a single panel or page, as in the opening of *Circle of Blood*, act 2, which I discussed in the introduction.

Such moments are made up of space that is assembled in a particular manner. This is why refrains are spatial elements—they connect motifs across collections and intensify their relations. That is to say, the repeated panel of the grave has an intensive effect that brings emphasis to this repetition in a way that does not occur for panels occurring only once. In that way, the grave panel features more prominently in the reading experience of *Kabuki* than panels that do not repeat. *Kabuki*'s comics assemblage is thus to a large extent organized around this refrain, this return to the death of Kabuki's mother. The extensive sequential narrative that each panel participates in becomes an intensive spatial form that participates in the construction of the melancholy mood of *Kabuki*.

For the refrain, what matters is not the next panel or moment but the return of the same moment as repetition. Sequentiality does not vanish but takes on a different function, where linkages are not contiguous but spread across collections, the same moment again, repeated without variation. The grave is always the same grave, the panel is always the same panel, Tsukiko's face is always the same face. Yet within the refrain lies the intensity of the repetition. The same returns without variation, but the return itself produces a degree of variation that manifests as a difference in intensity. Kabuki's first death is repeated in her second death, but where her first death tied her to Kai, her second death opens the journey away from Kai. The grave becomes the marker of the grief and loss of Tsukiko and so intensifies that grief and loss through its repetition without variation. The variation that does emerge, as is also evident by the growing space from the moment's return, is precisely the increasing distance to that intensity until it wanes into nothingness—the grave's complete absence in *The Alchemy*.

Let us unpack the usefulness of the refrain as an analytic concept. The first part of *Metamorphosis* is dominated by refrains that are also used to push the narrative of Kabuki forward. In *Metamorphosis* Kabuki continues to undergo her mental evaluation in the Noh institution. In *Skin Deep*, the preceding collection, she had made contact with Akemi through written notes. The doctor is unhappy about this, considering Akemi an imaginary friend. During the interview, Kabuki is asked to retell the story of her mother, which starts a restating of what was already covered in *Fear the Reaper* and *Circle of Blood*. The graphic style is different from the two earlier collections, however. *Metamorphosis*, along with *Skin Deep*, is part of Mack's shift toward full color. The images are done in varying formats but predominantly feature the use of crayons. Lines are generally clear but sometimes smudged, while at other times watercolor has been used to provide backgrounds. This graphic style is markedly different from the clear line black-and-white images of *Fear the Reaper* and *Circle of Blood*. In itself, this shift introduces a difference that underscores the variation in each repeated refrain.

The first page begins conventionally enough. A background drawing of Kabuki wearing her mask dominates the page, with one panel inserted in a different graphic style. The right-hand side of the page is taken up by seven small inserted panels, with the left-hand side being mostly captions from the doctor's log but with one panel of Kabuki. The next page immediately repeats the silhouetted shape of Tsukiko, this time in watercolor, kept in cool blues, greens, and grays. Kabuki slouches on a chair drawn in clear lines with handwriting giving information about her scars. A massive caption gives more information from the doctor's log but also provides a spatial counterpoint to the page layout.

There are three elements on the second page: Tsukiko's silhouette, Kabuki slouched in the chair, and the doctor's log caption. None seem to have a similar or associated duration. Tsukiko's silhouette is a burst of memory, recalled due to the Rorschach card shown to Kabuki. Kabuki in the chair has the duration of her dialogue, including the annotations of her scars. The log caption is dense and provides a lot of text, but it precedes the interview between the doctor and Kabuki. These three moments are spatially linked but have no immediate temporal association with each other. Although they follow in a chronological order of silhouette–doctor's log–Kabuki talking, they are not part of a causal chain. Their nonlinear locations are only brought into a linear sequence by narrative motivation. The doctor's log discloses the reason for showing Kabuki the cards: to understand if Kabuki is lying or imagining things. Kabuki's dialogue about her mother motivates Tsukiko's silhouette. Yet conventional reading direction dictates that Tsukiko's silhouette is encountered first, then the doctor's log, and finally Kabuki talking. While the reading order follows the chronological order of events, narrative motivation produces a different order. The page layout is simultaneously linear (chronologically on the level of story) and nonlinear (on the level of plot). We are given redundant story information before we know why.

Tsukiko's silhouette is the refrain, and this is the first time Tsukiko's silhouette has been repeated since page 73 of *Circle of Blood*, except for a partial recurrence on page 220. The return of Tsukiko's silhouette is surprising because so many other panels of Kabuki's mother have returned after far shorter intervals. The appearance of Tsukiko's silhouette sparks a series of repetitions that are all part of the refrain of Tsukiko's life and death. Panels and page compositions from earlier parts of *Fear the Reaper* and *Circle of Blood* are repeated in a complex interweaving of Kabuki's reminiscences and the doctor's interview of Kabuki. The interval between these repetitions is truncated, and most of the pages of the interview of Kabuki by the doctor are repeated panels and pages, repeated without changes except for the addition of color. Tsukiko's silhouette returns again in the interview (page 119), and the grave returns again in quick succession (124, 125).

The linkage to the earlier events is reinforced and intensified across the interview. The return of these haunting moments of sadness and grief is interspersed with several splash pages of Kabuki's upturned face (pages 113, 115, 116, 120, 124, 128). These spatial rhymes strongly link Kabuki's identity to her mother's death, but some of the faces are also echoes of Tsukiko, not Kabuki (122, 123), done in a way in which the similarity of the two faces blurs the distinction, precisely because of their spatial rhymes. Similar spatial positions integrate the two faces as part of a continuum, not as distinct identities but as continuations of each other. These rhymes inflect the thematic resonance that Kabuki also underlines in her interview: she is who she is because of who her mother was and how she was treated.

The repetition demarcates the narrative space with which the interview deals: the interview and Tsukiko. There is a double temporality marked out by the refrain: we are in both the time of the interview and the past. All the events have been narrated before; the moments reoccur within a slightly different sequence (several panels and pages are left out of Kabuki's recap), but the images remain the same.[12] The variation that is introduced with the repeated panels is on the level of trauma. Trauma repeats, and nothing repeats more in *Kabuki* than Tsukiko's death. There is a constant sense of afterwardness, of Kabuki trying to make sense of who she herself is, due to the return of her mother's death. Time comes back constantly and brings with it a new relation to the current situation.

The first time readers learned of Tsukiko, they received that information in the form of backstory. Kabuki's past and her origins were clarified and expanded, in the way that has become entirely standard for American superhero comics. A traumatic past is not at all unusual within this comics landscape.

Returning to an origin story is also not unusual. However, what we are dealing with here moves beyond the generic restating of the relatively static temporality of origin stories.[13] While any repetition of a panel or series and any change in position changes the meaning of a panel, what is emphasized here in *Kabuki* is the sameness of the moment. There is no mutation or rewriting of Kabuki's origin to make it fit into a new serial logic. These are the same events, underlined by the fact that the panels and pages are identical in composition. The back and forth temporal shifting, however, produces its own differential variation. One might be tempted to say that this is once more with feeling. I will return to the discussion of repetition and sameness in chapter 4, on rhythms.

What has been added is color. Whereas the interview has a white background, the refrain pages are full bleed, with color expanding across the pages, filling up the void. The memory permeates. Crayon coloring, watercolor, and graphic inserts of maps all produce a dense background that is mostly kept in rich, vibrant shades of orange, purple, and blue. The interview panels feel like an intrusion with their gray-blue washes and white speech bubbles. When we get to the doubly repeated panel of Kabuki as a girl on her mother's grave, the first instance is placed on the right-hand side, on the bottom. The right-hand side is dominated by a full-page image of Kabuki with her face upturned (itself a repetition, as noted) in a purple ink line drawing, itself the new addition to the panel. The left-hand side has sixteen panels of regular rectangles with a clear alteration in size: the first panel is the widest, and the subsequent panels then shrink. The final, sixteenth panel drops out of the regular grid, as a response to the doctor's question, "What happened to the girl?" All these panels are overlaid on the background of Kabuki's face and Tsukiko's grave, indicating that this final moment hovers in the background constantly and inevitably.

That inevitability and its impact are emphasized by a splash page repetition of Kabuki on her mother's grave. This time, colors are inverted, meaning that unlike the black image with white lines, it is now a white background with gray-purple ink, providing a sharp contrast with the richly colored preceding pages. A distorted panel of Kabuki is in the lower right-hand corner, indicating that time is passing. There is a jagged line that goes flat and continues flat over the next two pages, when the line becomes jagged again. This is Kabuki flatlining, only to revive again. Since the line continues across the full page of Kabuki on the grave, time is still passing. The moment, the terrible moment of Kabuki's death, is expanded and stretched, reinforced by the repeated panel until we reach the distorted panel of Kabuki saying "she died." The moment, that prolonged, awful moment, is over. Although the next few pages do include a few repeated panels, this panel is the shift away from the refrain and on to continuing the narrative development.

We see here how space intensifies all the different panel relations by bringing earlier events into proximity with each other. Again, while all these elements are visual, it is their (repeated) spatial relations that matter. The refrain of these repeated elements connects the disparate times and makes explicit the interrelation between Kabuki and Tsukiko. The page layouts spatially articulate the significance of the past through the use of the graphic refrains. This insistence of the interweaving of past and present, of memory and mourning, adds thematic richness and mood in the way that panels are repeated and become a constant part of the page background, although not the dominant narrative strand.

This is why rhymes produce mood. The repeated panels are all the same, but the sequence has been altered to intensify the relations between Tsukiko, Kai, and Kabuki. Although the general is present, he is less present than in the first iteration.

More important are color and time. The addition of color turns the moments into a pervasive and overwhelming expression. Time dilates in the moment of death, which is not an instant but a slow, protracted period of suffering. The first iteration was tragic; here the refrain transforms the moments into heartache. Succession is what guides this linkage between these moments and their return. The difference that this repetition makes is the introduction of a particular feeling. That feeling emerges as narrative mood in the subtle shifts in focalization. What was in the first instance an example of zero focalization becomes in this repetition internal focalization *without any change in the panels* but only in their external relations. The refrain is a concept that can grasp this transformation and express the difference it makes, underlining the linkage produced in the repetition, while also attending to the difference introduced. The shift in focalization, however, is far more important than I can deal with here, so I will return to it in chapter 3. For now, we can see the ways in which refrains become crucial to explicating and understanding the complex temporality of *Kabuki*.

Coda: Rhymes and Comics

This chapter has identified the usefulness of spatial rhymes in *Kabuki* in the two forms of linkage and refrain. Linkage deals with repetition and mood, rather than straightforward narrative. It connects motifs across panels, panels across pages, and pages across series in various forms of rhyming patterns. The refrain exists as a recurrent form that brings back a certain moment. In its repetition as difference, the refrain is distinct from flashbacks and flashforwards that place moments out of chronological sequence or restate earlier moments without altering the story. Although prolepsis and analepsis certainly do alter the experience of the story, the refrain is a form of repetition that links together non-narrative components and in so doing articulates mood and a complex coming-back of time. Alongside narrative time, or the unfolding of story, we find a different temporality, one of return and recollection that colors the narrative events. The tension between retention and repetition versus narrative progression is at the heart of the refrain as earlier events come back to have an impact on later events.

Spatial rhymes, then, link moments and motifs across the comics assemblage and in so doing produce mood. This chapter has argued that spatial rhymes complicate progression and retention in the way that graphic motifs repeat throughout collections and across collections. Linkages arrange something other than the spatial extension of the page layout: the logic of spatial intensities. The past of retention carries forward into the narrative progression and so through this repetition brings the graphic motifs closer together. This is why Groensteen's argument that rhyme is "distant repetition" is only partly correct. While there is clearly space between the repeated elements, their very repetition links them together and so makes the retention present, that is, not distant. While these links clearly depend on the reader's recollection, their function is evident: to bring close together that which is otherwise distant—and sometimes quite distant. By emphasizing the spatial poetics of comics, we begin to gain an understanding of the various functions of braiding that go beyond the minimal definition of nonlinear connections.

Kabuki is simply one example where spatial rhymes, linkages, and refrains are more prevalent. Yet, paying attention to spatial rhymes in any comic allows for a deeper understanding of how mood can be developed through the intensive connections between motifs. The mood generated by spatial rhymes develops in parallel with the narrative and inflects it in various directions. In *Kabuki* the constant return is the motif of the mother and the grave, suggestive of melancholia, grief, and loss. Much like the page layout cannot be changed without changing the expression of the comic, the spatial rhymes cannot change without changing the expression of the comic. The linkages do express intensity, but it is an intensity of mood over narrative progression. This recognition of mood as parallel to narrative opens up a different discussion of how space expresses time in comics. While there is a narrative progression, spatial rhymes enable a richer and more varied understanding of temporality than the standard discussion of transitions between panels. When time instead may fold into and across panels in the linkage plane, that time is no longer one-dimensional. Instead, there is a multiplicity of times and temporalities at work in the comics assemblage. This expression of time is what I will turn to in the following chapter.

2
Choreographies

Flows, Foldings, and Plasticities

Kabuki expresses a plasticity of time and space that is deeply connected to its narrative. Time is constantly revised, contracted, and expanded throughout the narrative episodes. Space, both in terms of diegetic location and in terms of page layout, is incessantly challenged. Such plasticity is intensified in *Kabuki*, especially in the issues that take place within dreams, hallucinations, or possibly schizophrenic episodes. Space becomes the main way in which these varying elements are expressed, and it also shows the dynamic nature of the otherwise static comics page. I want to explore this complex interaction as a means of escaping a rigid systematization that will never be able to capture the plasticity of space available in comics.

Time is notoriously difficult to grasp in comics, even though everyone agrees that there is only one way of expressing time in comics: space. "Time and space," claims Scott McCloud, "are one and the same."[1] Thierry Groensteen elides any fundamentalist statement on time in comics, referring to panels variously as "moments" or "fragments" of time, avoiding directly correlating space with time.[2] There is also the time that passes between each panel, which is certainly also a moment or fragment. As I will discuss in this chapter, comics do not exactly comprise "boxes of time."[3] Rather, time emerges as a spatial relation between panels, sequences, and pages. Conceiving time as emergent also helps us understand the relation between what Gérard Genette referred to as narrative time versus story time, especially as applied to comics by Julia Round. Genette's distinction is between the time of telling and the time of the told. As Round shows, the hybrid nature of the comics panel means that "a varying amount of story time" is expressed by panels and their relations.[4] This basic conception of time as variable allows for a flexible approach to the relation between narrative time and story time.

While it is relatively easy to describe the spatial extension of a panel (wide, narrow, tall, short, etc.) and its relational position (top, bottom, etc.), this does not hold true for time. We cannot with any certainty identify the temporal extension of a panel, a page, or even a collection. There may well be diegetic or extradiegetic markers of time ("meanwhile," "the next day," "ten years ago," and so on), but there need not be. I propose the term "choreographies" to indicate the interaction between time and space that comics perform. Although the term comes from dance notation, it is no stranger to comics studies. Art Spiegelman and Hillary Chute have both used the term.[5] More than that, choreography works well for comics because its original Greek meaning is "dance-writing," which suggests the notation of movement. This is accurate for comics—static images and words that express time as movement.

To get us started on the discussion of time in *Kabuki*, I return to *Fear the Reaper* and some of those early panels and pages that narrate Tsukiko's life. Page 47 opens with a panel of a sickle against the sun and the claw of a raptor. The page layout is regular, with two tiers of four panels. The six panels following the sickle–sun–raptor claw panel shift increasingly closer to Tsukiko as a girl, all the way to her eye, where we see the reflection of a man. Conventionally speaking, the argument would be that this page prolongs an intensely unpleasant moment. While there is a time shift between panels two and three, the rest of the panel shifts do not indicate temporal progression but function more akin to McCloud's aspect-to-aspect transitions. In one way, this turns McCloud's argument that time is space upside down. This page seems to say more space, less time.

McCloud would argue that this is an example of moment-to-moment transition, which requires little action to comprehend the temporal shift.[6] The final panel has the raptor claw above Tsukiko's head. Following McCloud's typology, this panel transition takes longer and requires more (though not much) action for the reader to comprehend. Yet there is a sense of stillness to this page that may as well be understood as a frozen moment in time in which story time does not progress, even as narration does. McCloud's transitions have little way of explaining this sense of stillness. Importantly, McCloud points to a sense of wandering contemplation in Japanese comics, which seems plausible inspiration for *Kabuki*. Yet there is more than contemplation at work in this expression of time. Narrational time is dislodged from story time; the reader is addressed directly and encouraged to see the causal connections between these panels rather than contemplate a mood.

Page 48 presents a different expression of time, and again there is a regular layout of two tiers of four panels. The first panel has faces in white against a black background with the caption "Her face is one in a frightened sea of faces." The next two panels have a Japanese soldier with a sword across both panels with a woman walking toward him, closer in the third panel than in the second. The fourth panel shows this woman up close, holding a jug. The fifth panel (and second strip) has a similar sword in the foreground but now held in the right hand instead of the left. In the background, a soldier grabs the woman, making her drop the jug. Panels six and seven show the jug closer to the ground, while the eighth and final panel shows the jug shattering against the ground.

This page layout plays around with time in subtle ways. The last four panels are a relatively traditional expression of time that shows a clearly defined action and event: the soldier grabs the woman, the woman drops the jug, the jug shatters. The narrative progression is legible, placing the final action at the end of the page, urging the reader to turn the page to see what happens next. The first four panels, however, are more difficult to parse. The first panel, of the faces receding into the distance, seems to not even depict an actual scene or event. Instead, this is a far more conceptual panel that seems to have a primarily indexical relation to what the caption expresses. The Ainu women were terrified of the invading Japanese soldiers and so presented a sea of frightened faces.[7]

This panel has no duration—it is not a moment, nor is it even an event that can be said to occur. It is an indexical expression of a conceptual fact: that these women were frightened for a long time. The panel is not timeless but presents an abstraction of time.[8] Because of this abstraction, the panel also does not have a determinable transition between the preceding panel (the raptor claw and Tsukiko's face) and the succeeding panel (the woman walking toward the soldier holding the sword). In fact, Tsukiko being scared of the soldier and the woman dropping the jug could easily be considered instances of the larger abstraction of the Ainu women being frightened of the Japanese soldiers. Considered this way, the panel of the frightened faces would be an abstracted duration that overlaps these two specific events and includes them both. Each panel contains its own duration, but, as a page relation, no connected time emerges. This notion of overlapping time will take on more relevance a little later.

For now, consider the last three panels of the top tier. The two middle panels may be understood as two slices of duration that show both stillness and movement. The separation of one composition into two panels suggests this interpretation. The composition is a Japanese soldier holding a sword in his left hand against a horizon of mountains that open to a plain. The two panels and gutter cut him into two successive moments, which is evident by the woman being closer to the soldier in the third panel. This is a completely conventional way of portraying duration and movement in comics; the sequence of panels suggests time passing. Unlike the last four panels, these two panels produce a tension between stillness and movement, precisely because two panels are used, rather than only one.

This leaves the fourth panel, which shows the frightened woman. More than expressing any particular slice of time, this panel shows the fright of the woman and so functions as a response to the frightened sea of faces that opened this page. Except for one panel that shows the reflected faces of the Japanese soldiers, these soldiers remain largely faceless across the page—once the soldier's head is out of one panel and in another, his face is cast in shadow because of his hat. The soldiers are unknown and expressionless, whereas the women have expressions. In other words, the fourth panel does not tell time but instead tells the plight of the Ainu women as an abstract duration. While the panel clearly exists in a direct temporal relation between the preceding and succeeding panels, the exact duration is hard to articulate. Once again, we can say that there is a time shift between the fourth panel and the preceding and succeeding ones.

"Time shift" is a term I take from Neil Cohn, who uses it without ever defining it.[9] Yet the term is intuitive enough that little definition is needed. Time, however we wish to measure or understand it, may shift inside panels, between panels, between pages, and so on. The crucial conditional for Cohn is "may," since we cannot be sure that time does shift simply because panels shift. In this manner, Cohn correctly rejects McCloud's notion that time is space, as well as Groensteen's argument that some extension of space changes into some other extension of time.

Cohn's argument is significant but brushes up against counterintuitive scenarios in comics, in which time never seems to pass. Cohn's argument is that some panels, such as locative panels that indicate a particular place, function outside sequential time.[10] Such panels would simply inform the reader of a location shift and do not contain any narrative time (although their inclusion would expand reading time). Similarly, consecutive panels might indicate the *same* moment from different perspectives rather than two different moments from different perspectives. This makes Cohn argue for event states or event frames—narrative unfoldings from which time emerges.[11] Time is not "on the page" as it were but inferred by a reader. Yet what is on the page are the potentials for inferring the expression of time, such as character pose, object position, background changes.

What we can take away from Cohn's argument is that a panel shift does not necessitate a time shift and that panels do not necessarily contain time. Sometimes, while time passes for the reader, no narrative time passes. The spatial rhymes discussed in the previous chapter, however, do suggest some temporal expression, even if it is not straightforward. Cohn's event states do not encompass or explain such time shifts, simply because some temporal shifts do not occur on the same temporal planes. Instead, a more plastic understanding of time is expressed, such as on page 49 of *Fear the Reaper*.

The shattered pieces of the jug from the preceding page resemble the Japanese islands, and in four panels in a regular layout, we see just how plastic comics' time shifts can be. The first panel shows the shattered pieces of the jug, while the second panel turns that outline into a black silhouette. The third panel is a drawing of the Japanese islands, and the fourth panel shows Ainu people working a field, with a flock of birds that rhyme with the shattered jug, silhouette, and Japanese islands. There is a running caption that informs us that the Ainu were driven north during feudal times to the island of Hokkaido, where they settled as farmers. A circular motif rhymes across the four panels. First, the liquid spilled from the shattered jug forms a circle that becomes the Japanese sun motif in the second panel, moved slightly upward. In the third panel, the circle is made up of small triangles around Hokkaido, and, in the fourth panel, the sun above the field is the circle.

What kinds of time shifts happen between these panels? It would be accurate to say that the first three panels have no duration at all, while the fourth panel indicates people working a field and birds flying, although that duration is hard to define. There is also no real event state at work here that would make us infer any causal link. McCloud's notion of a non sequitur transition seems affiliated, but the lack of duration goes against his argument. However, the caption does express a time frame: that of history. A historical time frame of decades and centuries across eight panels would suggest something along the lines of a temporal pace of summary panels, as discussed by Julia Round in her article "Visual Perspective and Narrative Voice in Comics." For Round, narrative time can be condensed, or made briefer than story time, through the compacting of panels as stand-ins for longer durations.[12] This is less an issue of time shifts than time compression, something signaled through the panel shifts of the page layout.

The first caption speaks of a family tree, suggestive of generational time, even if we only learn of Tsukiko. The caption continues, outlining how the Ainu people were driven north to Hokkaido to live as farmers. The circle motif moves north across all four panels, providing a spatial rhyme of upward/northward movement that parallels the forced migration of the Ainu. This is a temporal expression on a massive scale and not something that can be expressed as a panel transition or an event frame shifting, except for a long-running historical unfolding. The caption clearly anchors the shift from the Japanese islands to farmers in a field as being the Ainu, and the spatial rhyme of the circle transforming into the sun also provides coherence.

Yet the time frame shifts between the end state of an event frame from the preceding page (the shattered jug) to a historical process that took centuries (people moving north and becoming farmers, now working in a field). There is a massive temporal rewind between the jug and the Ainu people that shifts back to the time frame of Tsukiko and her people, across just four panels. These time frames are still connected, even if they are not presented in linear or chronological order; they are instead folded into each other. We can draw on Pierre Fresnault-Deruelle's argument about the linear and the tabular to suggest this complex temporal order. For Fresnault-Deruelle, the strip has a temporal dimension (the linear) while the page has a spatial dimension (the tabular).[13] The reader realizes the temporal interaction between linear and tabular expressions. What matters is that time emerges from the interaction of these linear and tabular expressions; time is not contained within each panel. Instead, linear and tabular aspects work together to express time.

For now, I will focus on the "problem of movement"—how does the experience of movement and the passage of time arise from static images? Choreography is a purely relational arrangement between panel, page, and series, and together they express the flows of time. For many comics, this flow will be predominantly narrative and so primarily linear, but this is a matter of convention and tradition more than a necessity. However, let us first examine how temporal flows of movement are established in *Kabuki*.

The Flow of Time

Skin Deep offers an opportunity to examine how choreographed space produces a flow of time. When beginning to read *Skin Deep*, the reader is immediately thrown into a temporal flux. There are three vertical panels, the first having an all dark-blue background reminiscent of some of the backgrounds in *Dreams*, then two black panels with screens filled with static and scratchy sound. The next page introduces an outline of a face against the static, scratchy dialogue: "I show you a card and you tell me what you see in it." The next pages alternate between panels of static and a dark-blue background showing Siamese, who have found Kabuki on the ground, dying. There is a sudden shift to four black-and-white line-drawn pages that have five vertical panels (two by two by one) that culminate in a splash page of a page and a half. The five panels are mosaics of earlier events in *Kabuki*—spatial rhymes mostly from *Circle of Blood*. This restating is accompanied by captions that provide a narrative summary. The splash page presents an overview of all the Noh agents, except Kabuki, with a host of toys and dolls that merge Western culture (Humpty Dumpty) and Japanese culture (manga-style characters and Godzilla).

The story shifts back to full-color pages and Siamese placing a bomb on Kabuki. Chronologically, *Skin Deep* follows *Dreams*, which told the story of Kabuki's near-death experience. Publication-wise, the collection is also after *Masks of the Noh*, a non-*Kabuki* spin-off series. Being presented with the twin Noh agents called Siamese, finding Kabuki, and destroying her corpse is therefore new story information that was not present in the previous collections. Neither *Dreams* nor *Masks of the Noh* indicates that Siamese discovered Kabuki. Temporal flow, however, is relatively straightforward. Each alternating panel introduces a degree of simultaneity; there is a temporal relation between the two different temporal lines that the reader does not fully know. After the recap of black-and-white pages, the alternating panels recede and each panel shows new story information of Siamese discovering Kabuki's body, shooting at the Kai agents, and calling back to the Noh. There are no motion lines, although there is gun muzzle fire, indicating action. However, often the panels will show Siamese in the same position, with dialogue being what indicates temporal passage. All in all, it is a hectic, fast-paced sequence in which time is choreographed spatially through spatial shifts (both in terms of the page layout and visual perspective). Time flows across the pages linearly. Fresnault-Deruelle's linear-tabular relation is instructive again: the tabular function keeps the reader moving toward the next page. The last panel of a page sets up curiosity to make the reader turn to the next page.

Like so: page 27 starts with Siamese talking about Kabuki while loading a gun and ends with one of them firing that gun. Page 28 shows them both shooting, with one of them being hit, and ends with the other pulling her sister back. Page 29 shows the one sister shooting, while dragging her sister, and ends with the body of Kabuki getting smaller, indicating that Siamese are leaving. Page 30 shifts closer to Kabuki again as the bomb's countdown reaches zero and it explodes. This tabular function creates a rhythm of payoff-setup, in which we get the conclusion at the top of each page and the cliffhanger at the bottom. There is a linear spatial flow across the panels that emphasizes this temporal flow.

This is a typical action-oriented page layout. Although this is indeed an action-filled scene in the sense of a gunfight, what I am getting at here is action as the progression of narrative. Events follow each other in clear, linear fashion, each smaller event (shooting, speaking, pulling) arranged into a larger event (fighting Kai's agents who are trying to kill Kabuki). Time emerges from this flow as narrative movement: one panel after the next, one action after the next, one event after the next. The differential relations between each panel, between each page, indicate that characters have moved, that events have occurred. Through that string of causality, movement is choreographed (although the panels remain static) and time flows. Temporal flow may be a hectic time, condensed and breathless, or it may be slow, measured time. What matters is the process of differential relations. Each new panel changes, even if it is only its position on the page that changes.

This is why the linear-tabular relation must be understood as a process, not a static structure. This process between linear and tabular spatial arrangement is the choreography of time. Fresnault-Deruelle may not exactly argue this way, but I want to suggest that reading a comics page flows between a tabular sense of the entire page simultaneously with the linear sequence. This back-and-forth flow informs the reading flow in terms of which panel to read next, while at the same time explaining each panel in its larger spatial arrangement. It is in this way that the linear-tabular distinction flows together in a meaningful process. And it is through this back-and-forth process that temporal flow emerges from space as a choreography of durations.

Tom Gunning calls such flow of time a "graphic speedup," when "the images increasingly present phases of a continuous action[, and] . . . gaps between individual images become briefer."[14] Gunning's notion is clearly related to McCloud's moment-to-moment and action-to-action transition. We can instead argue that in terms of expressing movement, rather than producing a typology (helpful as that may be), the smaller the differential relations are, the less time appears to pass. Yet "appears to" remains crucial, since there are instances when time may contract or dilate in ways that have little to do with (temporal) gaps between panels.

A good example is page 54 of *Skin Deep*—a splash page that appears to have very little action (Kabuki paints her cell). With the amount of detail fit within the panel, however, it may take a long time to move to the next panel.[15] This would be one example of a graphic slowdown, though page 67, for example, which technically has only four vertical panels, is also an instance of graphic slowdown, due to the amount of written text in each panel. The falling origami animals, each representing a new letter to Kabuki, do indicate a longer passage of time as well, and so the inferred temporal gaps dilate. These splash pages show the tension between narrative time and story time well. The amount of detail indicates a slowdown of reading, but page 54 can also be regarded as a summary panel—the fact that Kabuki is in the process of painting her cell indicates that much time has been spent painting the rest of her cell. While the splash page can be read as the moment of her having reached this point in painting her cell (making the duration of time in the panel relatively brief), it can certainly also be read as a summary of the entire event, making the story time much longer.

Whatever speed the pages generate, time is choreographed as a flow in which events follow neatly after each other. Time passes, however fast or slow, according to the spatial flow of each page. Movement emerges from the differential relations between panels and pages (and series). The greater the difference between each panel, the greater the potential for a longer time shift, though this speaks only to the pace of each individual narrative event. Events fold into each other to form larger events that eventually fold into the full narrative of an issue, then a collection, then a series run. As long as events follow from each other, as long as there is conventional causality in each panel shift, time is choreographed as movement. Whether these event shifts are fast or slow, moment-to-moment, action-to-action, or something else is irrelevant to the flow of time. Narrative

force moves along linearly and even event shifts between past and present (flashbacks, memories, etc.) do not break the flow of this narrative force. Certain linear-tabular arrangements render the narrative pace fast or slow. This speed, that speed. But that is a discussion for a later chapter.

The Folding of Time

The idea of folding is necessary for understanding the panel relations of *Kabuki*, not only for the pages just discussed but also for pages 51 and 52, along with many other page layouts across the entire run of *Fear the Reaper*. Pages 51 and 52 will serve as my final discussion of the complicated temporal expression in *Fear the Reaper* before I set forth a theoretical discussion that is up to the task of analyzing these temporal expressions and putting them to the test with an analysis of *Skin Deep*.

Page 51 is a splash page of Tsukiko as a grown woman with a decorative insert panel of General Kai. The narration caption relates how Kai made the Ainu women perform kabuki plays and that he never violated them or allowed his soldiers to do so. The narration is what produces a long-running duration of several months if not years of the Ainu women performing these plays, and the panel simply expresses a character relation. This page repeats as a panel insert on page 52. Page 52 is a splash page that consists of several spatial rhymes from earlier pages. The top-left corner has the sun and the flock of birds that rhyme with the panels of the sun and birds on page 49. The top-right corner has a bird on a branch that rhymes with the bird on page 50, even in the same spatial location. The middle has the previous page as a panel insert on a black background, with the top of that black background turning into barbed wire that then turns into the birds in the top-left

3. *Kabuki: Skin Deep*, 54.

corner. The bottom has the moon in the night sky and Tsukiko in her kabuki costume and makeup, crying the single tear that repeats on Kabuki's mask. Tsukiko's face and the moon rhyme with Kabuki's mask on page 53, the final page of *Fear the Reaper*.

The spatial rhymes produce coherence but also bring multiple temporalities into one page, without a sequence emerging. The sun-and-birds rhyme brings in the Ainu farmers and indicates a collective time, not Tsukiko's own time in particular. The bird-on-the-branch rhyme comes from the kabuki performances ordered by General Kai but is an earlier event than the bottom of the panel. The inserted panel repeats the previous page and brings in the time frame of General Kai and Tsukiko's relationship. The bottom part of the page is the first new story information on the page and depicts a performance in which Tsukiko is crying.

There are thus four time frames that are not of the same order, nor do they switch between each other in any meaningful way. Better to understand them as simultaneously caught up in the expression of Tsukiko, her relation to Kai, and her relation to Kabuki (and Kabuki's relation to her mother). Page 52 alternates between these two dimensions and suggests that there are several temporal dimensions that converge in this spatial dimension. These different times fold into the same space, without any degree of time shifting to suggest a generative event state. Choreographed space, understood in this manner, becomes highly complex and can express more than direct panel transitions.

Chute has developed the concept of the comics page as offering "a rich temporal map configured as much by what isn't drawn as by what is: it is highly conscious of the artificiality of its selective borders, which diagram the page into an arrangement of encapsulated moments."[16] Chute's definition works well to describe page 52 (and many others in *Kabuki*), with the possible problematic of "encapsulated moments." Her earlier phrasing in the same article—"complex, often nonlinear paths across the space of the page"—is better because that leaves out the notion that panels contain time. Panels do not contain time; time emerges from panel-page choreographies. The relation between panels and page is the choreography of time and is what Fresnault-Deruelle's linear-tabular argument also gets at—the way that panels are arranged is the choreography of time because the part-whole relation emerges through that interaction.

Cohn protests against the temporal map for two reasons: first, that panels are moments, which we can see does not necessarily follow from the idea of a temporal map, and second, that "all spatial relations must then have temporal consequences."[17] This is a problem for Cohn because such consequences cannot be easily quantified. This is not an actual problem, though, because no one has said that the idea of a temporal map indicates that *all* spatial relations must have temporal consequences. Space may well choreograph time while also expressing other aspects. Spatial rhymes would be just such an instance. The spatial rhyme of the bird on the branch, say, does not mean that time has passed for the bird on that branch. The rhyme simply recalls that panel, and while that rhyme is spatial, it is not temporal.

The temporal map, then, should be understood not as a mapping of consecutive or nonconsecutive moments but rather as the choreography of time. In fact, as is also evident from page 52, there is not necessarily one timeframe at work in comics. There may be multiple temporalities that fold into each other and express a complex choreography of temporal relations. Chute argues as much when she remarks on "the ability of comics to spatially juxtapose (and overlay) past and present and future moments on the page."[18] This overlaying, or what I prefer to call folding, may even occur within a single panel. Folding is preferable since it suggests multiplicities that are in themselves plastic and may wrap around each other. Furthermore, folding does not indicate any obstruction in the way overlaying does. Temporal folds proliferate in *Kabuki*, even within the relatively straightforward volume of *Fear the Reaper*.

Let us move away from regarding the temporal map as stringing together boxes of time and instead consider Fresnault-Deruelle's linear-tabular concept as a choreography that arranges panels, page layout, and series into temporal relations. This choreography is necessarily spatial, since comics are static and whatever they express must be expressed spatially. To say that this choreography is static is not to imply that there is no formal interaction between panel, pages, and even collections. Juxtaposition, folding, and other spatial arrangements are what allow temporal expressions to be formed—that is to say, spatial forms carry potentials for time shifts. Although the reader realizes these time shifts, this does not suggest that any kind or type of time shifts may be realized. Spatial forms guide and constrain the realization of these time shifts as much as they open them up.

Regarding the panel, sequence, page, and series as maps of choreographed time, we sidestep questions of any direct correlation between spatial extension and temporal extension. In this view, no longer are panels "boxes of time," nor are pages sequences of linear or tabular time. Instead, the comics assemblage of panel, page, and series is the choreography of time. These choreographies express time through spatial means. And more than one time may be expressed: not linear, not nonlinear, but a folding together of a multiplicity of times simultaneously. This is one of the properties of the comics medium that stems from the interaction of linear and tabular page design. While most often used only to express a linear flow of time, choreography holds many more potentials.

The Plasticity of Time

Folding multiple temporalities into one panel or page means that we have to understand time as far more flexible than a linear flow of movement, even with the nonlinear devices of flashback and flashforward. Time, in the comics assemblage, can be choreographed in far more intricate patterns, with several layers of time. Multiple moments may be choreographed together across the comics page and so create resonances that go beyond plot arrangement. Conventionally, time in comics is seen as either sequential or durational.[19] However, for *Kabuki*, time should be considered as plastic—a malleable material that may be rendered spatially in a wide variety of ways.

This is so in the case of the layout of page 41 of *Skin Deep*. This page has panels, but it can also be considered a full-page layout. The page depicts Kabuki and the doctor in a therapy session, with several overlaid and jagged versions of Kabuki in her mask and only one depiction of the doctor. There is geometric juxtaposition and mirroring between Kabuki in the top-left corner and the doctor in the bottom-right corner: their spatial opposition is suggestive (and productive) of their general antagonism. The splintering of the panels into jagged shards also suggests Kabuki's state of mind.

As should be evident, the spatial extension of the page layout is complicated, yet the temporal flow across these panels is complex; the panels' rhyme, mirroring, and ambiguous contents produce a graphic slowdown. There is little explicit movement here, both in terms of character movement and narrative movement. Kabuki and the doctor simply sit across from each other, talking. The complex choreography of the panels, however, requires readers to slow down their reading flow and navigate the different relations between panels and the temporal flow that is expressed here. The slowdown comes

from the discrepancy between story time and reading time. Reading time is expanded beyond story time, because readers cannot simply immerse themselves into the dialogue flow but have to reflect on the spatial arrangements of panels and connections and how that spatial form contributes to the story.

There is dialogue here that suggests a degree of temporal progression. Kabuki asks if other agents went rogue, to which the doctor answers affirmatively, saying that many Noh agents lose touch with reality due to the many false identities they have to assume as part of their missions: some crack, some experience trauma, some go insane. The many faces of Kabuki may be regarded as expressive of her many different identities, the ways in which she cracks. The shattered panel that tellingly starts with the face of Kabuki may also be understood in this manner: Kabuki has cracked and her identity has shattered. This would fall well in line with the overarching theme of mental trauma and strained identity, as well as the narrative and visual allusions to *Alice in Wonderland* that run throughout the series though most explicitly in the earlier collections. The allusions to *Alice in Wonderland* emphasize the dream-like nature and hallucinatory aspects of many of Kabuki's experiences. Not only is Kabuki a pawn in the earlier collections, later on her authority as narrator is constantly questioned.

So, in this way, the page layout may simply be regarded as expressive of the narrative concerns. While correct, this is not satisfactory either. The page layout does not simply clarify an appropriate reading regime or a particular interpretation of the panels.[20] While the captions of the doctor's words do provide a reading direction, the panels themselves are difficult to place within any kind of temporal flow. They do not depict narrative events per se but rather belong to Kabuki's thoughts,

---

4. *Kabuki: Skin Deep*, 41.

the flow of her experience. In relation to time, it should by now be evident that time is plastic here. We do not know how much time passes or what the temporal relation between the different panels is. This is exacerbated because many of the panels contain only part of Kabuki, the rest clearly continued after the gutter. Does time shift? Perhaps, but the four top left panels probably do not shift very much, whereas the top right panels do not seem to express time at all.

We can identify three temporal flows: the dialogue between Kabuki and the doctor, the dilation of time in Kabuki's experience of feeling strain on her identity, and a third, quite subtle flow of words that are not exactly on either of the two other temporal planes. Running across the page are strings of words that belong to Kabuki. They are not in regular captions or boxes but flow along the margin of the page, the outline of Kabuki's body, falling along the shards and punctuating the lips of one of the faces of Kabuki. This punctuation is the word "mother," which does not seem to belong in the same flow as Kabuki's comment on reality being merely a word on her lips. And yet, of course, "mother" is Kabuki's reality and is literally on her lips. But this running commentary does not exist on the same narrative level as that of the dialogue between Kabuki and the doctor. Instead, it belongs to a narrative position chronologically *after* their meeting.

To reiterate, there are three temporalities on the page: the narrative flow of the conversation, in many ways the main temporal flow; the flow of Kabuki's experience, her thoughts about what the doctor says about other Noh agents; and finally the flow of words that indicate another level of Kabuki's experience but from a different temporal position. These words have a sense of the afterward about them, as if she reflects on the page and sequence itself. These temporal flows fold together as spatial forms. Time is rearranged into these three separate, if not entirely distinct, flows that connect and fold together, not one time but multiple times, while arranged on the same spatial plane.

In his dissection of *Hellboy*, Scott Bukatman suggests the concept of "pillow panels," where panels present contemplation rather than sequential narrative time.[21] We find here another instance of how time is a complex matter in comics. Bukatman's idea of pillow panels suggests not so much a graphic slowdown as a suspension of story time to allow the reader to absorb the panel. There is a contrast to cinema here that needs addressed. Time moves outside of viewer behavior in cinema (barring the use of pause buttons and the like), and so the duration of shots and editing styles largely guides the attention of the viewer. For comics, any panel may be contemplated for as long as the reader desires, since the story will not progress without reader activity. Yet Bukatman's point stands, since some panels do not further narrative action but provide moments of mood.

Contemplation and stillness are not the cases for *Kabuki* on pages such as the one discussed here (although one can certainly contemplate the artwork). Instead, time is molded in part by Kabuki's experience of time, rather than by the flow of narrative time. The collection *Skin Deep* depends on this form of design, in which panels and pages take on highly subjective dimensions. The collection as a whole focuses on Kabuki's mental state, alluding to her possible breakdown and loss of identity. Allusions to *Alice in Wonderland* and *Through the Looking-Glass* are evident in dialogue (e.g., "a looking-glass into hell" on page 22) and in the jumble of comic book characters on a double splash page that shows Humpty Dumpty and Kabuki's Cheshire cat alarm clock, all of which continue from *Circle of Blood*. These allusions suggest a mental breakdown, but more so than this continuation it is the constant oscillation between narrative time and subjective time—Kabuki's experience of time.

The linear choreography of time that expresses movement and action through differential relations between panels and pages is molded by the folding in of Kabuki's subjective time. Consider the opening I used earlier as an example of the flow of time. We can now see that *Skin Deep* opens with Kabuki thinking back on being rescued by Siamese. The staticky panels show the doctor (a character we have not been introduced to before) and the Rorschach test that she gives Kabuki. However, we will not see the Rorschach test being administered until the next collection, *Metamorphosis*. The rescue is new information that does not connect with what has previously been published. The alternating panels of Siamese and the staticky panels take on new significance, not simply as staticky images but as scrambled memories, perhaps. And the progression of the narrative also casts some doubt on the status of Siamese encountering Kabuki. Kabuki is unconscious and dying—how can she remember Siamese? And more to the point, how did Kabuki survive the bomb blast? There is a degree of unreliability that will become important later on.

That these are memories is evident by the captions associated with Kabuki waking up after the bomb panel. First, she lies in bed in the same fetal position as in the panel before the bomb blast. The spatial rhyme between these two panels (even if across five panels and three pages) links the two and seems to suggest that this was more a dream than a memory. Second, she thinks, "Rewind again. That was now. This is then." Even what appears to be the present is signaled as being in the past. Kabuki's unreliability as narrator is pushed to the forefront, so much so that the communication with Akemi may easily be regarded as hallucinatory. This is especially so when Kabuki hears the voice of Mika, whom she realizes serves the Control Corps, the people who keep her imprisoned. Maybe, Kabuki speculates, Akemi also works for the Control Corps.

The fact remains that we do not know, although it is strongly suggested that Kabuki is suffering from a mental breakdown. Even when she encounters Akemi face to face, there are clues as to this encounter being unreliable. This unreliability does not manifest solely on the level of story but is also expressed in the spatial design.

On page 97 of *Skin Deep* Kabuki talks to Kageko, another inmate. The Control Corps will train her to take on Kabuki's identity, having learned her way of moving and her mannerisms. Kageko will even be given a mask identical to Kabuki's, only made to fit her (Kageko's) face. The page layout has a light to dark purple background of smeared color, lighter in the top-right corner, darker in the bottom left. A pencil sketch of Kabuki is placed in each of two corners, thus mirroring each other. The middle of the page is taken up by about twenty inserted panels that all overlap, obscuring each other. The panels are mostly different angles of Kageko's face in black-and-white illustrations. There are three full-color panels of Kabuki's mask, one panel of an inverted color line drawing of a face, and a panel of what looks like a desaturated photo of a face. The sketch of Kabuki on the bottom right has a panel around her face with "ME" written in it, just below a panel of Kageko's face with "YOU" written in it.

This layout illustrates well the topic of their conversation— masks, faces, and identities. Kageko's face is as fragmented as her identity; she must be both herself and Kabuki at the same time. Time is here deformed. There is no sense of linear time flowing; this is not one event that folds into another event to form narrative flow. Even a tabular view of the page provides little temporal flow. There is a time shift between the top sketch of Kabuki, the middle panels of Kageko, and the bottom sketch of Kabuki, signaled most clearly by the dialogue. But the proliferation of panels and the fact that none of them provides a full view of Kageko but instead only a composite when taken together does not suggest time shifts at all. There is a sense of stillness spread over multiple perspectives to suggest a subjective time, the time of Kabuki's experience. The multiple panels also express the fragmented identity of Kageko, in an expressive function of the page layout.

The plasticity of time expresses the instabilities of the Noh agents' identities. They struggle with being in the present moment, sliding between past and present (and future), while the narration and focalization also slip and slide between different levels. This subjective component of time is pushed to the forefront in the collection *Dreams*, which functions almost entirely as deep access to Kabuki's subjective experience of dying. This notion of subjective access and how deep that is will be discussed further in the next chapter.

After the austere black-and-white design of *Fear the Reaper* and *Circle of Blood*, the collection *Dreams* comes across as an explosion of wild stylistic experimentation. Full-color painting, watercolors, photographic inserts, and collages all add up to a plethora of visual expressions that bear almost no resemblance to the two earlier collections. The story of *Dreams* is quite minimalist in terms of narrative progression but rich in subjective experience. *Dreams* can be understood as Kabuki's experience of the time between page 244 of *Circle of Blood* and page 15 (the first page of the story) of *Skin Deep*.

Dreams reaches into *Skin Deep* because of the words "beep beep beep" scrawled across the two final panels of *Dreams*. This is new information not present in *Circle of Blood* and not motivated from within the story of *Dreams*. We do not see Kabuki being revived in *Dreams*; the only indication that she survives is the sequence of beeps in the panels. These beeps are the external world slowly intruding into Kabuki's mind. My point here is that *Dreams* does not function as a conventional sequel that fits between *Circle of Blood* and *Skin Deep*. Most of *Dreams* actually restates the events of *Circle of Blood* internally and concludes with the opening of *Skin Deep*; Kabuki emerges from her death-coma back into consciousness.

This shift from consciousness to death-coma and back to consciousness is expressed through the visual and material transformation of Mack's style and opens up his shift toward a far more expressive graphic style, in terms of both graphic design and narrative design (such as the subtle shifts in focalization mentioned above). Along with the shifts in graphic style, there is also a shift away from panel gridding to more free-form and decorative page layouts. This shift is necessitated by the plastic choreography of time as the focalization shifts inward to register Kabuki's internal experience of time, rather than the external narrative unfolding. The linear and tabular interactions become increasingly complex. One of the tensions that arises between the linear and tabular dimensions of the page layout is what Charles Hatfield terms the "surface." This surface is both the sequence of page layout and the page as an object.[22] That object has materiality—both its "size, shape, binding, paper, and printing" and also its "design or layout."[23] For *Kabuki*, this shift in materiality comes in the form of a wide variety of mixed-media experimentation.

On the double splash page 309 of *Dreams* we find massive layering of various materials. A busy background filled with strips of paper, lines, and peonies is filled with different colors and drops of paint. Leaves, butterflies, peonies, and digitally produced paneling in bright colors dominate the left side, while darker colors dominate the right side. There are five panels on this page, but they are inserts of sorts. These panels are foregrounded not only through their prominence but also through their design. They catch the eye, especially on the

5. *Kabuki: Dreams*, 309.

right side of the splash page due to the color contrast against the gray-brown and black background.

In and of itself, the page's layering produces spatial tension through the different visual expressions. The blurry digital photo inserts barely look like photographs, and we really only recognize them as such due to earlier panels in the same collection. There is a color rhyme of reds, oranges, and yellows from the blurry digital photo inserted into the paper art collage. This reinforces the association between Kabuki and Tsukiko, makes the shift between the two inserts easier, and also makes this linkage the dominant one for the page. The final photo insert is far darker and makes it recede toward the background, even as it is placed in the foreground. The use of photographs to depict a character that we otherwise associate with a specific illustration style (from *Fear the Reaper* and *Circle of Blood*) is complicated because of the photography's far greater realism. Still, the photos do not exactly look like Kabuki, since readers identify Kabuki as an illustrated character.

How much time passes on this page? On the one hand, there is no particular sense that time passes between the inserts and the page as a whole. Words are floating around on the page, but there is not enough information to suggest narrative flow. The first and last insert are so different that we may hesitate to see them as part of the same sequence. Reading direction is also challenged, for while the decoration of the first panel makes us intuitively begin there, it is not clear if we should read toward the right or toward the bottom. Neither panel flows more organically from the first. Instead, the second and fourth panels (counting from left to right) do seem to be linked, even if a sense of progression is hard to maintain. The panel with Tsukiko and young Kabuki is meant to link with the dominant panel, since both panels have the same characters in them.

This difficult progression is further challenged by the insert in the right-bottom corner. Emerging from the background and in a black-and-white palette, this insert is layered over by the more vibrant colors of the panels, making the insert fade and go almost unnoticed. Alongside the highly fragmented background, the splash page may well be a single moment (moments have duration, of course) or multiple moments folded together. The shift in graphic style between each panel may then be suggestive of time shifts, even if this is not particularly clear.

However, once we understand the splash page in relation to the rest of the issue, the relation between panel and page becomes somewhat clearer. This issue of *Dreams* opens with several panels of black-and-white photos of Kabuki. The tension between the splash page's vibrantly colored panels and the dark background insert becomes one of not just background and foreground but one of external and internal focalization—the vibrant colors express Kabuki's dreams, hallucinations, or near-death experience, whatever the case exactly may be. The shift in graphic style thus emerges from the material components that have gone into producing the surface of the page. That surface in itself takes on a particular feel, which produces a sense of time, as we realize that each panel expresses different moments in Kabuki's life *as dream*. There is no linear time here, nor is there exactly a distortion of time that expresses only Kabuki's impressions. Instead, there is a simultaneity of time. All these different parts of Kabuki's life come tumbling back to her at the same time, as another plastic expression of time.

Although this splash page carries relatively little narrative information, the time to read it (or at least take in the information) lengthens due to the various materialities; time slows down and the splash page requires a much longer reading duration. The same holds true for the noncaption writing that weaves around the splash page. Although always associated with panels, the writing does not obey any one orientation. Instead, the reader has to twist and turn the comic to read the words. This also makes the comic into a physical object because it becomes an object that the reader must literally handle. We are confronted with the need to turn the object in our hands (or crane our necks) or ignore story information.

Time is densely folded, not in a chronological order and not solely a subjective thing. Through its complex interplay of foreground and background, *Dreams* evokes three dimensions, not simply two, as is the norm for the vast majority of comics. For *Dreams* this third dimension renders time visible as a fold—not a line but a three-dimensional space, where one moment touches other moments. This is most easily done in a part of the comic that deals with Kabuki's inner experience of her life. Yet from this point on in the entire *Kabuki* series, Mack manipulates time through the manipulation of space in a far more free-form and plastic way. This is the plasticity of time—folding, layering, and materially; time is choreographed as a mélange of many different temporalities and moments that exist simultaneously on the comics page.

Coda: Choreographies in Comics

Time and space are thoroughly entangled for comics, and this is true for *Kabuki* as well. What *Kabuki* tells us, however, is that there is no direct formula for the passage of time based on space; there is no objective correlation between space and time, even if they are expressed together. Typologies such as McCloud's transitions may be helpful in many cases, but space is far more plastic than any system may encompass. Spatial extension does not translate directly to duration. Instead, the notion of choreography is much more attuned to the way that comics can express time in many different ways—ways that are not simply sequential or durational. Time shifts, but that does not always mean that time passes. To say that time dances on the comics page may be slightly too poetic for academic purposes, yet there is a distinct choreography in how movement and action are expressed on the page. In a similar way, due to the interaction of panel and page, time is not necessarily singular in comics but can be multiple.

As we have seen in *Kabuki*, there are many different spatial strategies for organizing events on the comics page. Spatial rhymes are ways of linking elements that produce narrative cohesion but do not necessarily suggest duration. Spatial rhymes do, however, have the capacity to bring in multiple temporalities by associating one event with another, or even by repeating one event during another event. Thus, time may fold spatially into other times. Panels and sequence runs may also fold multiple times into each other through various complex panel-sequence-page interactions, whether we think of these as linear-tabular arrangements or surface tensions that may layer these temporalities rather than organize them sequentially. This is the way, then, that space choreographs time: spatial arrangement and spatial shifts allow for time shifts to be realized by readers.

I have identified three primary spatial forms of time—flow, folding, and plasticity. We should keep in mind that these forms are tendencies and so should not be considered as fully distinct. They swirl into each other, one form or another being dominant at different times. The flow of time is both physical and narrative movement. Characters and objects change across panels, which indicates that some amount of movement has occurred. Linear flow of time is a narrative convention in most comics and is also what inspired McCloud's transition typology and similar ideas of space equaling duration. This is not to say that the flow of time is somehow simplistic. Even though the flow of time is driven by both actions and events, it may still be nonchronological and flashbacks may still occur. While uncomplicated, the choreography of time may still be complex, understood as the dynamic, shifting, and evolving relations between panels, sequences, pages, and so on. The premise for the flow of time is an articulated set of causally linked events, all of which work together to produce a stable flow of time. Physical movement, narrative action, and character behavior are intelligibly laid out on the page, and time shifts are legibly marked through changes in panels. The relations between linear and tabular are well defined and flow in unambiguous patterns. Regular grids often, though by no means always, express an intelligible flow of time and in a way more complex than a straightforward idea of space equaling time.

Folding occurs when multiple temporalities are brought together in the panel or on the page. The folding of time remains a spatial expression, since the sequentiality of panels does not easily break down into time shifts. Even sequentiality is challenged, since at times the reading sequence is ambiguous. There is here an association between the disruption of spatial flow (do we read from left to right or from top to bottom?) that to some extent mirrors the disruption of temporal flow (does this panel shift to a later event, a past event, or a parallel event?). Association is not correlation, so the suggestion is not that we can explicitly decode a ratio of space to time, only that spatial relations choreograph temporal relations. Different temporalities coexisting may produce rich resonances. Joe Sacco shows how the past remains present through the use of folding in his *Footnotes in Gaza*.[24] As a character explains how he escaped armed guards, a split panel traces his arm in a single position. Temporally, however, the first panel is in the present of the telling, while the second panel is in the past of the told. By using a split panel, the folding together of past and present is emphasized through a spatial arrangement. Similar temporal foldings are used in Grant Morrison and Chris Burnham's *Nameless*, where a combination of split panels and inserts shows the same location in two different moments.[25]

Plasticity, then, is way of expressing time that comics may employ in a way quite different from other media. By folding multiple temporalities together, time can be choreographed in highly unusual ways. For *Kabuki* this is done in two dominant ways—the subjectivity of temporal experience and the complication of story time. I will investigate this complication of story time in the next two chapters.

"Choreography" is the best term for bringing together these different spatial forms of expressing time. Everything is brought together in a dynamic interaction of components across panels and pages, and although this relation is static, its realization is temporal. We simply need to keep in mind that there is not just one time but several temporalities and that they interact and entangle in many different ways in comics. Furthermore, as the word "choreography" is meant to make clear, temporality is always expressed spatially in comics but in a dynamic manner that readers apprehend in the absence of any direct correlation between space and time.

3
Perspectives

Graphiation, Knots, and Positioning

As is now evident, *Kabuki* contains many scenes that are dreams and hallucinations. While we have seen the kind of impact this reverie state has on the depiction of time's passage, these dreams, hallucinations, and other mental distortions also impact narration and its relation to focalization and point of view. Such narrational issues are closely connected with issues of spatial form. In comics, spatial positioning is expressed quite literally in the perspective of images. Spatial narration may also be understood more figuratively, both in terms of the depth and width of narration and also in relation to the narrator position within the diegesis.

There are several issues here that overlap yet need to be clarified. The first is the role of Kabuki as narrator and of narration versus graphiation (which is to say the tension between the plot and the graphic style of the plot). The second issue is a concern with focalization and the knowledge that we gain about story, character, and world. Much of this knowledge is complicated by being spatially knotted through more than one point of view. That brings us to the third issue, which is literal point of view—from whose perspective do we see the events unfolding? Spatial point of view is a necessary part of all comics—events are always shown from a particular perspective and position.

In *Kabuki* spatial perspective is often rendered ambiguous by splitting who sees from who narrates.

Narrator Shifts

In the previous chapter, I devoted a lot of space to discussions of time shifts—incremental, often sequential shifts in time between panels. Here, I wish to make an argument about a similar shift between panels, except this is not an issue of time but of narrator shifts. Many ensemble comics (such as *X-Men* or *Watchmen*) employ narrator shifts to provide access to each character in turn. Other comics shift between narrators to provide broader knowledge of the story. This means we need to distinguish between heterodiegetic narrators—who are outside of the story proper—and homodiegetic narrators—who are part of the story being told.[1] For comics, this distinction is complicated by being a matter of not only who tells the story but also whose spatial perspective we inhabit.

The main change between *Skin Deep* and *Metamorphosis* comes at the level of narration, not narrative. Whereas *Skin Deep* opens with heterodiegetic narration and then slowly changes to Kabuki as homodiegetic narrator, *Metamorphosis* immediately plunges into full-on tension between heterodiegetic narration and homodiegetic narration, by both Kabuki, who may be suffering from delusions, and the doctor. Furthermore, it is not unusual for the narrator function to be deemphasized so that the question of the narrator never comes to the fore. The situation is different for *Kabuki*, in which the narrator shifts and is pushed into the foreground.

Narrator shifts also open up a discussion of what Kai Mikkonen calls the "agent of narration."[2] Mikkonen chooses this slightly awkward phrase because of comics' tendency toward third-person, non-character-bound narration. More simply, comics can have narration that is not tied to a character. Unlike literature, where narrator position is necessarily part of the linguistic enunciation, comics' visual construction does not include a narrator in the same apparent way. Karin Kukkonen has suggested that rather than film's "deus absconditus" narrator, there are "traces of narration" evident in panel compositions, page layouts, drawing styles, and so forth—all the aesthetic devices of comics.[3] This distinction between narration and narrator is strongly attenuated in *Kabuki*, precisely as an ambiguity of who enunciates the narrative events.[4]

The two opening pages of *Metamorphosis*, discussed earlier, reveal these narrational tensions. The first page has Kabuki's face, in her mask, looking upward. Deep purple ink lines form the background to a predominantly white left side and a right side filled with panels, alternating between Kabuki's face and the doctor. There are many blue-colored captions, beginning with "Doctor's log. Case 2001" and continuing with the doctor's comments on Kabuki's case and mental state. The dialogue is sparse and kept in white speech balloons. The doctor shows Kabuki a Rorschach card; the last panel of the page shows it to us with the caption "What do you see?" This indicates, as is also evident a few panels earlier, that the doctor's notes have turned into her dialogue. While the doctor is visible in a panel, we get her dialogue as a white speech balloon. If she is not in the panel, her dialogue is in a blue caption. There is an elision between notes (written after or possibly during the session) and dialogue that is quite subtle on the level of narration, yet there is a time shift of blue-captioned notes that fix the panels as depicting actions that have already happened. If the blue-captioned notes are in the present, then the narrated event must have already happened, since notes are written afterward. But as the blue captions shift to dialogue, the events unfold in the present, casting the doctor's notes as somehow subsequent to the events we read.

Next page. There are two overlapping panels, with the top-left one a spatial rhyme of Tsukiko in her kabuki costume with the jade statue overlaid on that panel. A frameless panel of Kabuki slouched in a chair takes up the bottom right of the page, overlapping the panel of Tsukiko and the jade statue. Kabuki's response to the Rorschach card is in a white speech balloon in the top-left panel. The top right of the page has a blue-captioned note from the doctor, yet again subsequent to the event that we have read. Kabuki's panel has several handwritten notes detailing her injuries and scars ("worst scars under mask," "stitches from Kai's sword," "scars on arm from preppy ninja," and similar information).

While seemingly a spatially simple page, the narrational levels are quite convoluted. The top-left panel is focalized through Kabuki, since Tsukiko is not actually there, being merely a memory jogged by the Rorschach card. This is made clearer not only by the sequence from the preceding page but also by Kabuki's speech balloons and body overlapping with that panel. That dialogue clearly belongs to Kabuki, and the blue caption (although temporally disjointed) clearly belongs to the doctor. That leaves the handwritten notes informing us about Kabuki's injuries. Although the notes are in blue, the color is deeper and richer than the doctor's caption notes, and so we cannot ascribe these notes to the doctor. One of the notes indicates that they belong to Kabuki: "Gunshot wound from Noh security. Control Corps removed 9ft of shredded intestines and stapled me up." This would indicate that Kabuki relates this information but certainly not to the doctor, since it is not part of the dialogue. That means that this is narration for the reader and thus is part of a running commentary from Kabuki, on another narrational level than the current narrative event of the therapy session.

As is so often the case, *Metamorphosis* includes a recap

of Kabuki's backstory, especially a discussion of her mother Tsukiko's story. After the two opening pages, already discussed, Kabuki tells the doctor of her mother's life. Immediately, this registers as a change in graphic style. The colors change, from cooler blues and purples to warmer, redder hues, and the number of panels immediately increases as well. The layout itself is significant, however, as there are several split panels. Mostly a grid of six-by-three panels, the top tier of six panels is Kabuki's masked face, rhyming from the face on the opening page—turned upward and looking out from the top-right corner of the page. The next split panels show Kabuki sitting, and they consist of four panels, gridded—two horizontal and two vertical. This leaves four middle panels that form a sequence with the five bottom panels below them of Tsukiko as a child. Whether the split panels of Kabuki disrupt the narrative flow or simply mark a different reading flow depends on individual realization.

However, the four-plus-four panels of Tsukiko as a child have their own spatial arrangement, irrespective of how we read the sequence. The last four bottom panels are tilted at increasing angles, suggestive of falling. The background of these falling panels itself has drawings that intrude. While the left side of the page merely has a rich, deep blue background suggestive of a somber mood, the bottom-right corner has a dark, sandy beige with distinct black drawings and purple written words: "disunite," "seperate [sic]," "disjoin." The drawing is hard to decipher but appears to be a woman's face and possible coastlines on a map. This is verified on the next page, where the same drawing is reproduced as foreground but without the written words.

What does this page tell us in terms of narration? At first glance, the page layout seems quite straightforward, and despite the use of split panels, the reading flow appears easy. The tilted panels are also easy to read; their angled tilt rhymes with the falling jug in the panels, while the suggestion of falling correlates with the fear that young Tsukiko evidently feels. However, a closer look at the panels reveals that these are repetitions from *Fear the Reaper*, pages 48 and 49. While they are not literal reproductions but redrawings and the first two bottom panels in the sequence are new, the young woman dropping a jug and the shards transforming into a map of Japan are easily recognizable. This is the same narrative information and events that we already know.

In other words, this looks like a flashback. Yet, this is not entirely correct either. The narrative events and information may well be the same, but the visual and spatial expressions are different. The drawing style is different, Tsukiko looks slightly younger, the panels are colored, and the tilted angles are new. That is to say, the narrative content is the same, but the narration is different. In some ways, this was always already the case in *Fear the Reaper*. While that was the first time we were told of these events, they were clearly marked as Kabuki's narration, not Tsukiko's or a third-person, non-character-bound narration. Before the flashback to Tsukiko's childhood, Kabuki is at her mother's grave and reflects on her life, narrating that "my consciousness widens to take in this drama of the mind" and, continuing, that "it has been well-rehearsed and finely-tuned with age." In other words, this is told from Kabuki's perspective. This is also the case in *Metamorphosis*, which is why the variations in the repeated panels are not continuity errors but rather express a change in Kabuki's mind.

The panel compositions' spatial alterations, as well as the spatial changes in sequence, position, and angle, are functions of a narrator shift. Although these panels are narrated by the same character, there is a shift in that character-narrator. This is not unique to this single page but continues across the next ten pages, culminating unsurprisingly in a full page of young

Kabuki dying on her mother's grave. While these eleven pages function as a recap of already established narrative knowledge, these repeated panels are also variations—not simply based on their content, at times redrawn, at times reproduced exactly, but based on their spatial arrangement. Some details that the serial reader already knows have been omitted here, while others are kept in place but made smaller so as to fit on the page. Page 123 of *Metamorphosis*, for instance, reproduces most of the panels on pages 85, 86, and 87 from *Fear the Reaper*, but they are now condensed into a single page, not through omission but by making the panels smaller.

To be clear, there is a narrator at work in these pages, not simply a depersonalized narration. This is clearly cued in the opening page of the flashback with the emphasis of the split panels of Kabuki. She is marked as the narrator of what follows, and everything is focalized through her knowledge of her mother's life, imperfect as it may be. This is one narrator shift expressed spatially through the split panels and through the variations of the repeated panels and their alteration in graphic style. The agent of narration is evident through this change in graphic style. Rather than being expressed on the level of linguistic enunciation, the narrator shift occurs on the level of graphic enunciation.

Graphiation as Spatialized Narration

Here it makes sense to bring in the idea of graphiation. There has been extensive discussion about the concept of graphiation as necessary to distinguish between *what* is drawn and *how* it is drawn. Originating in comics studies with Philippe Marion, "graphiation" is part of a dual set of terms, the other being "monstration." Monstration comes from André Gaudreault's work on cinematic storytelling, which he splits into narration and monstration. Narration, for Gaudreault, is editing whereas monstration is actor-character behavior.[5] In film theory Gaudreault's conception is overly idiosyncratic, so I will not discuss it further. Marion takes Gaudreault's term and splits it into two: monstration and graphiation. Monstration, for Marion, are the figures, objects, and other parts of the storyworld—that which we use to understand the story—or everything, as Thierry Groensteen puts it, that has been rendered "into graphic form."[6] Graphiation, however, is the often overlooked aspect of the artist's individual style—the thickness of the line, the choice of colors, and so forth. It is everything, we might say, of the drawn form's rendering. This includes composition, layout, and similar spatial forms, since all these aspects remain part of how comics (and artists) express story, character, and world.

Although the distinction between the monstration of what is drawn and the graphiation of how it is drawn may appear quite subtle, the idea of style goes quite some way toward explaining reader preferences for certain artists in comics where writer and illustrator are not the same. Furthermore, the distinction also allows for close attention to how narration shifts may be expressed through changes in style.

Mikkonen has argued that the term "graphiation," while popular in French comics theory, is not necessarily better than the term "graphic style," which he understands to be "lines, traces, and graphic design, used in both images and lettering."[7] While I am loath to prolong this already lengthy theoretical tangent, a distinction between graphiation and graphic style may be useful in maintaining an emphasis on issues of narration and narrator. That is to say, the narrator shift that we experience in the opening of *Metamorphosis* is best termed graphiation, since it deals with the dispersal of story information from a particular narrator. While this is certainly a matter of shift in the graphic style, it impacts the question of narration. Indeed, the narrational shift is marked by the change in graphiation.

For example, once the flashback sequence is finished, we enter back into the therapy session's back-and-forth pattern. While this narrator shift puts us back in the present, we now see information that can only come from Kabuki. On page 129, Kabuki sits in the same position as earlier, indicating that only a short period of time has passed, despite the passing of several pages in terms of plot. Gone is the top-left panel of Tsukiko and the jade statue. Instead, orange origami animals form a semicircle that concludes in an orange panel of Akemi's face. Outside that panel, the rest of Akemi stands behind Kabuki, though clearly only in Kabuki's mind. The superimposed Kabuki reclining in the chair is one of Akemi's notes, telling Kabuki not to trust the Control Corps. This relationship was fully developed in *Skin Deep*, and in the therapy session Kabuki tells the doctor that Akemi is not real, although Kabuki herself believes she is. This presents another narrator shift, if only in terms of tense—a return to the present from the flashback to the past.

At the same time, however, the page layout spatializes multiple channels of narrative information. Akemi standing behind Kabuki, the origami animals, the notes from Akemi are all information given to the reader, not to the doctor. That means that there are in fact two narrators simultaneously at work on this page. The first is Kabuki as a personalized narrator, homodiegetically narrating her life, experiences, and knowledge to the doctor. The second is Kabuki as personalized narrator, heterodiegetically narrating events to the reader. Significantly, these two narrators *are not the same narrator*, nor are they even entirely the same character, since they are distinct in terms of narrative progression—same character but at different points in the story.

The first narrator is a homodiegetic narrator, who within the story itself narrates a different part of the story, a part that has already occurred and that we as readers are assumed to know. This narratorial instance is suggestive of present-tense narration—this is what occurs right now between Kabuki and the doctor. The second narrator is heterodiegetic and narrating from a position *after* and *outside* the present-tense narrative between Kabuki and the doctor. This is an instance of temporal folding; there are two temporalities that are spatially folded together on the same page. Again, this is graphiation—the dispersal of narrative information through graphic style, yes, but also through page layout. It is not simply the thickness of the line, its curve, or its color but the arrangement of narrative events across a particular spatial formation.

Graphiation, then, also associates with characterization what Shlomith Rimmon-Kenan terms a reinforcement device. A reinforcement device is when something external to a character nonetheless reinforces that character's personality or behavior. This can be achieved in a number of ways, such as weather, landscape, names, and so forth.[8] Essentially, any aspect that does not directly signal character traits may still reinforce them through metaphor and other devices. For some famous examples from literature, consider that the gloomy, crumbling Castle Udolpho personifies Signor Montoni's villainy or that the old man Santiago's struggle to catch a marlin is a metaphor for pride and ambition. In the same way, Gotham and Metropolis are aspects of Batman's and Superman's personalities as much as they are expressive of the comics' different atmospheres.

Rimmon-Kenan, dealing only with literature, cannot discuss graphic style, since this is such a marginal practice in the literary field. In comics, however, graphic style certainly plays a part in expressing character. Character design is one obvious way and is present in all comics, but with *Kabuki* all shifts in graphiation are achieved through changes in graphic style. These changes also register on the level of character, something also found in *Masks of the Noh*, in which each of the different Noh agents is drawn by a different artist. With the choice to assign a different artist for each character, the change in graphic style also changes the mood and feel of each character, adding to characterization.

A different example of narrator shift is evoked in *Metamorphosis* with a repeated panel (in fact a single splash page). Page 130 is a direct reproduction of page 105 of *Skin Deep*, except for an inserted panel of the doctor telling Kabuki that this image is an intercepted transmission. Its placement here is significant, since it is presented as new information to Kabuki, while it is redundant information for readers of *Skin Deep*. The splash page is the last page of *Skin Deep* and concludes three important pages.

The three pages are rare instances in the *Kabuki* series of a narrator shift away from Kabuki. Page 103 opens with a large panel of Kabuki that takes up most of the top-left part of the page. This is the beginning of a therapy session, in which Kabuki reiterates word for word what she stated (as a caption) in *Fear the Reaper*: "My consciousness widens to take in this drama of the mind." Here it exists as part of the dialogue between Kabuki and the doctor. The rest of the page consists of twelve small panels, the first two shifting to a surveillance room, where we see Kabuki on screens connected to surveillance cameras. Two bored guards watch these screens as Kabuki continues repeating the words from *Fear the Reaper*: "It has been well-rehearsed and finely tuned with age." The next eight panels show one of the guards leaving for the bathroom and the second one sitting and waiting, watching the screen as someone else—Scarab—walks up behind him and cuts his throat.

Scarab lets other Noh agents in, and they confirm that they have located Kabuki. Around the page frame run the words "Our mission is simple. . . . Find Kabuki. If she's dead, bring back her corpse. If she's alive, bring back her corpse." These words are repeated from earlier in the series, once again emphasizing the temporal dislocation of *Kabuki*. The most relevant aspect of these three last pages is the subtle narrator shift away from Kabuki's first-person personalized narrator to a third-person, nonpersonalized narrator. We can make an argument that the narration shifts to Scarab, yet she does not have access to what the two guards say. In other words, from being a highly subjective narration with deep access to Kabuki's thoughts and feelings, the narrator shifts to a nonpersonalized narrator with little access to any character's subjective experience. That this happens almost unnoticeably is a testament to how flexible narration works in comics. This unnoticeability also goes some way toward explaining why spatial perspective is so often overlooked; when not accentuated explicitly by the comics narration, it recedes into the background.

Narrator shifts are done spatially; they are signaled with panel transitions but also through page layouts, color alterations, drawing styles, and other, similar graphic style changes. Since comics quite rarely employ subjective point-of-view perspectives, we are used to seeing characters who narrate in the panels. This means that the presence of a character does not indicate whether that character also functions as a narrator or if there are any narrator shifts associated with them. Careful analysis is often needed to untangle such narrator shifts, simply due to the plasticity of comics narration. "Graphiation" is a good supplementary term for articulating this separate narrative plane.

Focalization as Spatial Form

What happens when there are two points of view in the same panel? While I will explore this literal idea of spatial perspective a little later, I will first engage with the question of focalization and its spatial expression. While narrator and focalizer are quite close, there are differences. Focalization may best be understood as "knowledge of the storyworld," as Kukkonen puts it.[9] We can easily think of narrators who do not necessarily have deep knowledge of story, character, or world. Autobiographical comics such as Alison Bechdel's *Fun Home* often necessarily resort to speculation or invention in terms of guessing other people's thoughts and feelings. Such examples are instances of narrators with limited knowledge of story, characters, and world or simply with shallow focalization.

The question of focalization is crucial for *Kabuki*, especially because focalization is deep in terms of access to Kabuki and her experiences. As already discussed, *Dreams* may largely be considered a plunge into the depths of Kabuki's mind. We have the same narrator as in *Circle of Blood* but much deeper focalization in *Dreams*'s repetition of events. Here we see another aspect of how spatial form complicates our understanding of page layout—the depth of focalization as a dimension of character access. I do not mean to psychologize the characters here and argue for some Freudian depth structure of characters' minds. Instead, I draw on the canonical formulation of David Bordwell and the depth of narrative knowledge that a narrative may convey.[10] The more subjective the knowledge that is communicated, the deeper the focalization is.

In *Skin Deep* and *Metamorphosis*, deeper focalization is pushed to an extreme through the use of spatial form. On page 65 of *Skin Deep*, perspectival position is doubled so that the same panel contains two visual perspectives at the same time. The page has two tall, vertical panels. These panels follow a page of eight panels with distorted, warped lines that indicate the mental strain on Kabuki as a result of being isolated. The first panel has two focal points. The first is a close-up of Kabuki's face looking at an origami angelfish, while the second is Kabuki in full figure, standing up and looking down on the origami angelfish.

The most immediate, and less accurate, reading of this panel is to follow it sequentially, as two separate moments kept in the same panel. However, this argument would overlook the fact that the sequence is reversed. Kabuki would first see the angelfish on the floor and then pick it up to look at it, not the other way around. Furthermore, such a reading would also disconnect the prior page sequences of Kabuki's already confused perception. It seems better to me to argue that the narration turns these two distinct and separate moments into a doubled moment—Kabuki's perception is confused and foggy, so she cannot separate the two sequential moments from each other. On one level, this is simply a matter of plot and story distinction. On the level of story, Kabuki obviously saw the angelfish on the floor and then picked it up to look at it, but on the other level this does not represent the plot as it is expressed. And this spatial expression is deliberate, a way of expressing Kabuki's subjective experience of being under mental strain.

This example shows us how the depth of focalization, or how much access we get to Kabuki's subjectivity, is accomplished through the spatial form of overlapping perspectives. A visual perspective always requires a vantage point, and here multiple spatial vantage points are overlaid without being congruent with one another. This particular form is another instance of how spatial relations take on significance over the visual. The page does not produce a conventional sequence but instead disrupts temporal flow through a spatial construction. Space is what communicates the depth of access to Kabuki and her emotional state. Perspectival vantage point, overlapping images, and a hierarchical organization of story elements are all part of the page's layout.

6. *Kabuki: Skin Deep*, 65.

When we argue that subjectivity is expressed in a particular manner, we are back to a discussion of graphiation and graphic style, even as we enter into slightly different territory. For the vast majority of comics theorists, style, especially drawing style and graphic style, is a matter of the "mark of the maker."[11] This is intuitively true. Most comics artists tend to find a distinctive visual style, and this is especially true of those comics creators associated with one writer-artist, such as Frank Miller's work on *Sin City* (though not all his work), Alison Bechdel's *Fun Home*, and Chris Ware's works. David Mack has chosen a different approach—his style changes and adapts across the series. Certainly other artists do the same. Consider J. H. Williams III's quite different artwork in *Promethea* (written by Alan Moore, 1999–2005) and *The Sandman: Overture* (written by Neil Gaiman, 2013–15).

In this way, graphic style (and not only graphiation) becomes a matter of subjective character experience. That is to say, graphic style is not tied solely to Mack's personal illustration style and so is no longer simply a mark of the maker. This is not an argument against Mack having a recognizable style, different from other comics artists' styles. He does and it is. More crucially, though, he employs a range of different graphic styles as means of expressing character thoughts and feelings. As briefly noted in the introduction, he is not alone in this. Works by Bill Sienkiewicz and Sam Kieth are the clearest examples of such deliberate alterations that go beyond stylistic experimentation or development. Instead, all three artists use graphic style alterations as an aesthetic device to express character subjectivity, especially in terms of deep focalization, that is, character thoughts and feelings.

An example of the use of graphic style shifts to suggest focalization alongside access to a character's subjectivity occurs when Kabuki and Akemi sit in the bathtub, after Akemi has knocked the guards unconscious. Kabuki talks about being imprisoned and then Akemi asks, "What's it look like inside your cocoon?" in the last panel of page 145. That page and the preceding six pages of the second part of *Metamorphosis* are done in Mack's default style at this point in his career—full watercolor, kept in deep blues and rich purples, quite realistic in graphic representation. The pages are generally gridded with few panels; there is no real symmetry, but we see on the whole balanced layouts and legible spatial flow.

So it is a shock when turning to page 146, which is a single splash page with an insert in the top-left corner. The color palette is mostly bright yellows and light beiges, with small pale blue, light red, and white squares for background. The drawing style, however, is childlike, via crayon: a bright yellow sun with a slight smile and visible rays coming off it, an outline of a boat on the water in blue crayon, two stick figures in the boat. A stick fish in red smiles up at the two people. The insert panel is done in the same child-like style, although with a deep blue background. The bathtub has turned into a boat, with Akemi and Kabuki sailing together. An inverted S-shape line of written text in black reads, "I told her about my mother . . . the comfort women . . . about a little girl's face being cut up . . . bleeding to death . . . I've talked of those things . . . but I was thinking of folded messages . . . red penned words . . . brightly colored sculpted paper . . . that take me back to childhood memories." These words recap the narrative events of much of *Skin Deep*, but that is not what they signify. The words and especially their graphic style signify Kabuki's child-like personality, as well as her reminiscing about her childhood. This is not a narrator shift but another plunge into the depths of Kabuki's mind—we get deeper access to her subjectivity through this graphic style shift.

Mikkonen identifies such shifts in graphic style as functions of "mind style," which produces "cues of a character's mental set or world view and, moreover, . . . interpret[s] these markers in relation to an evolving frame of consciousness."[12] Mikkonen's argument is sound, but in order for it to be entirely accurate in this case, the preceding pages of *Metamorphosis* would have to have had zero focalization—no access to character thoughts or feelings. We do not shift between narrators marked by different mind styles but remain with the same narrator. There are several cues for those pages being focalized by Kabuki. Page 142, for instance, has a narrator relating information alongside body outlines, along the water pipes, and so on.

At the same time, Mikkonen is not wrong, either—the graphic style shift does signal a shift in mind style. We go deeper into Kabuki's mind, and so the shift in graphic style should be regarded, in this case at least, as an intensifier—a spatial cue that we are moving deeper into Kabuki's memories and feelings about her past. Keep in mind that the sun and fish are both smiling, indicating that the situation with Akemi must be understood as pleasant, despite the traumatic memories that bubble to the surface. What is presented and how it is presented serve as cues for how to understand not only the narrative events but also how Kabuki feels about these narrative events. A graphic style shift suggests what Mikkonen calls a "means of characterization," through the current emotional state of Kabuki.[13]

How is graphic style a spatial form? As we can see, the conventional way of discussing graphic style is to say it is a matter of appearance. The mark of the maker typically speaks to line thickness, color choice, choice of graphic representation, and so forth. Indeed, I have discussed Mack's style in such terms above. But there is also a spatial aspect to an artist's graphic style. This is most classically discussed in terms of gridding. Choice of page layout has a huge impact on narrative construction and reading flow and may be strongly connected with a given work—such as the tight, regular gridding of *Watchmen*—or an artist's storytelling—such as Hergé's regular gridding in his *Tintin* series.

Mack rarely uses regular gridding, though he develops a proclivity for collage-style layering of visual elements and producing a multitude of different shapes that organize narrative information, such as the S shape mentioned above and the tiger flow discussed in the first chapter. In the next chapter, I turn to the ways in which page layouts develop rhythm. For now, I wish to stick with the way that perspective and spatial arrangement work to provide narrative information.

Kukkonen has remarked how visual representation of fictional minds is often difficult to sustain in comics, as "images are usually perceived for what they show, not the perspective from which they show it."[14] This is certainly one of the reasons why comics so often are thought of in terms of third-person, non-character-bound focalization—images tend to be understood as objective, seen from an external perspective.

However, *Kabuki* uses spatial arrangements to suggest internal perspective, letting the space of the page layout focalize differently (and deeper). The location on the page signals different instances of focalization, just as changes in gridding and page layouts are indicative of character access. This is one of the ways, then, in which Mack's spatial form allows for subjective access and narrative knowledge. By arranging narrative information in what are essentially different layers of focalization, spatial form becomes the primary way that we gain access to Kabuki.

The intensive shifts in graphic style that Mack constantly deploys in *Kabuki* serve as spatial cues for focalization shifts. Let us unpack this argument to see how space works. First off, the intensive shifts in graphic style indicate that each change is a change in experiential quality; this is the argument of graphiation. Second, because these shifts are instances of expressing the

emotive component of the character-focalizer, these changes in graphic style grant deeper access to character subjectivity—an argument that hinges on a spatial metaphor. Lastly, how then are these changes in graphic style spatial cues rather than visual cues? Again, it is because each graphic style is a particular way of organizing space—the space within the panel and the space of the page layout, as well as the connections and associations of the sequence and assemblage of panels across pages. In other words, each graphic style has its own form of spatial arrangement, its own way of organizing space to express character emotion.

Furthermore, the exact nature of the graphic style should be considered in relation to these focalization shifts. That is to say, in the example above, the child-like crayon drawings are suggestive of childhood memories and feelings, whereas the previous style has marked itself as conventional for this collection. Style is relational, in the sense that it is the change that signifies. These focalization shifts are different from narrator shifts, since these are not necessarily shifts from one narrator to another. Narrator shifts should instead be associated with a width of narration, whereas focalization shifts should be associated with depth of narration instead. Both of these terms are organized spatially in the comics assemblage.

Knotting Focalization

How then are these shifts generated spatially? Page 154 of *Metamorphosis* presents a good example of spatially generated narrator and focalization shifts. Kabuki has told Akemi the story of her childhood goldfish Mizuko and how Mizuko died. General Kai wants her to accept the death and flush Mizuko down the drain. Ukiko (Kabuki as a child) believes

---

7. *Kabuki: Metamorphosis*, 154.

that Mizuko will come back to life just as she herself did. The page layout has three panels, of sorts. Split down the middle, with the left side being white and the right side in deep blue with full bleed to the edge, the page has one panel at the top left and one panel on the right a little farther down, which is essentially an insert in the last panel, which can be construed as the entire blue side of the page.

In essence, there are three levels of focalization at work on this one page: (1) the center panel of Ukiko flushing her goldfish, which may be spatially anchored to General Kai; (2) the bottom panel of Mizuko in the ocean, which is Ukiko's imagined narrative; and (3) the top panel of Mizuko the goldfish, which literally has the mark of Ukiko the maker and so is her explicit focalization. These shifts exist at three different depths of focalization: (1) Ukiko's experience, (2) Ukiko's imagination, and (3) Ukiko's feelings about losing her goldfish. The shifts in graphic style are what cue readers to these different depths of focalization, not just mind style or character, since the panels are all the same mind and same character. These three levels align with Rimmon-Kenan's three facets of focalization: Ukiko's experience is perceptual, her imagination is psychological, and her feelings are essentially ideological, in the sense that she evaluates her world and the general's actions.[15]

Furthermore, this page is also an excellent example of how these three levels of focalization are spatially dependent. The fact that they overlap shows that all three levels are part of the same character's subjectivity and that they are interconnected. The panels fold three temporalities into each other, but spatially each duration is distinct yet impinges on the others. We can distinguish between story space and spatial presentation as a way of separating the narrative space (within which the story takes place) from the spatial composition of the page.[16] The panels show three different times but also three different spaces; their locations matter, but more than that it is their spatial form that expresses their relation to each other. Here we again find a foreground-background effect, although this time in the form of a layering effect of different story lines literally overlapping, being spatially contingent.

Spatial form in this context suggests that focalization itself is spatial, when multiple perspectives exist within the same panel. In this instance, unlike the literal spatial perspectives that combine in the example above, the multiple perspectives are focalizations of different depths. These three different levels of focalization are not separable by character or narrator, since they all belong to the same character-narrator. Instead, a slightly different term is needed. I use the term "knotting" to indicate different levels of focalization from the same narrator. Knotting is similar to temporal folds, except that knotting brings multiple perspectives together on the same panel or page.

In *Kabuki* focalization is knotted to an extreme in relation to several of the inmates at Control Corps. As Kabuki and Akemi attempt to escape from Control Corps, they enlist the help of several other inmates. Each inmate gets a splash page to express who they are—sometimes a double, sometimes a single page. Take Ann as an example. In a splash page, we see her cell and her self-portraits. The page is overlaid with some form of design, but we can only tell that it has small squares with faces on a mainly black background with a lacy design. There are no panels here, although there are clearly multiple spatial perspectives. This makes for a somewhat messy and confusing splash page.

Kabuki as narrator has several captions running across the page, explaining that Ann has so many identities that she has forgotten who she is. Instead, she draws portraits of herself "in an attempt to recognize herself." Along the baseboards of Ann's cell walls run the words "She swipes our Scrabble

pieces to incorporate into her art." We know that "our" refers to Kabuki and Akemi, and so that possessive pronoun anchors the narrator of those words. While the two versions of Ann in her cell clearly mark two distinct moments, the rest of the page does not have any distinct expression of time. The two portrait sketches are necessarily simultaneous. Ann has made them before Kabuki and Akemi encounter her, and so they are not part of a temporal sequence but only part of the focalization.

When we understand focalization as anchored less in a given narrator or character and more in story knowledge, we can also see how focalization knots on this page. There are several markers of focalization that indicate they are separate. First of all, neither Kabuki nor Akemi is present anywhere on the panel, except as the origin of Kabuki's captions and the words along the baseboards. In itself, this is hardly unusual, since a focalizer need not be visibly present. But as is also evident from the page layout, there are multiple spatial perspectives on the page. The two versions of Ann indicate the same spatial perspective, only separated by time. But the two portrait sketches each represent their own spatial perspective, existing simultaneously on the page—no frame to separate them, no reason to think they are temporally distinct. The writing along the baseboards is clearly nondiegetic, not part of the world or visible to Ann or anyone else. They belong to focalization and give us access to Ann's actions. Kabuki's captions are clearly marked as hers and provide narrative information as well. But despite the captions and the baseboard writing both originating from Kabuki as narrator, they cannot belong to the same level of focalization, since they are graphically distinct. The baseboard writing is easy to miss in an initial read-through,

---

8. *Kabuki: Metamorphosis*, 178.

whereas the captions are not. In other words, the narrative information is not distributed evenly.

What does this mean? It means that there are five levels of focalization at work on this page, yet they are all knotted together into what *appears* to be zero focalization but is in fact distinct levels that knot together. The two portrait sketches are focalized by Ann; this is how she sees herself in whatever moment she drew them. They are not identical, so they suggest different views of the same person, which is congruent with her multiple personality disorder. The sketches belong to Ann and no other character (or focalizer) because their graphic expression is part of her identities. This follows from my earlier argument about graphic style—that drawing style is expressive of character identity. Thus, we cannot attribute those sketches to any other character. The section of the two versions of Ann cannot be attributed to Ann, since she renders herself differently. While we could argue that this is a point-of-view perspective from Kabuki or Akemi, this is probably the clearest instance of zero focalization on this page, as long as we do not include the baseboard writing. The captions running across the page are attached to Kabuki, since only she would have access to this knowledge and in this way. We can see this in the way she says, "I'm told she's drawing her self portrait," thus marking her own narrative knowledge.

The captions are then internally focalized, which would also seem to be the case for the baseboard writing. Yet again, these two levels of focalization are not identical. The captions are neutral, not just because they follow standard comics conventions of narration but also because their square boxes and blue color have been established as typical throughout the collection. This does not hold true for the baseboard writing, which belongs to the other category of written narration; as I pointed out earlier, it is not unusual to find writing appearing along object and character outlines in *Kabuki*. The level of focalization in these writings exists in tension with the captions. The most obvious indication of this is the graphic variation between the two. The captions are standardized, while the outline writings generally vary in style and are always handwritten.[17] For that reason, the graphic style is what marks the baseboard writing as a different level of focalization.

With this different focalization level, a parallel is established between Ann and Kabuki. A running concern throughout the entire series has been Kabuki's mental stability. The recurrent allusions to *Alice in Wonderland* and *Through the Looking-Glass* that have appeared since the earliest *Kabuki* collections have suggested this theme since the first collection, and collections such as *Dreams*, *Skin Deep*, and now *Metamorphosis*, with the Control Corps story line, have pushed this idea into the foreground. There is no singular answer to the question of Kabuki's mental state, since almost all of the series is narrated from her position, making it difficult to distinguish between actual events and hallucinated events. However, let me briefly defer that issue and instead turn to the last instance of focalization on the page—the Scrabble tiles in the upper-left corner. Read vertically, they spell "Who am I," a question that applies equally to Ann and to Kabuki. Only with the baseboard writing do we understand that the words to belong to Ann, since that writing anchors the tiles.

Let's summarize this pregnant page. On one splash page we find no fewer than five levels of focalization, none of which readily suggests time shifts or narrator shifts. Focalization does shift, however, and provides us with different depths of story, character, and world knowledge. These shifts are expressed spatially through a juxtaposition that does not entail temporal progression. With the exception of the two versions of Ann, there is no indication of time passing. The sequentiality of the page remains, yet it expresses different depths and widths of knowledge. Similar examples occur when broad overviews of story elements are presented, such as page 48 of *The Sandman: Overture*, where many different forces are presented in a splash page, or page 9 of volume 3 of *Something Is Killing the Children*, by James Tynion IV and Werther Dell'Edera (2021), where multiple characters are shown in different panels, with monsters approaching outside.

Knotting indicates how different levels of focalization are rendered visible on the comics page; it is a form of juxtaposition and sequentiality that differs from narrative and temporal unfolding but adds depth and breadth of knowledge about story, character, and world. While there are shifts, these shifts are often hard to recognize immediately, and they tend to resemble zero focalization. On closer inspection, however, it becomes clear that several different levels are present on the same page. We should not assume that knotted focalization occurs only on splash pages, however. Page 191 of *Metamorphosis* has four panels, two of which are inserts, yet we find the same complex knotting of levels of focalization on this page, the shifts in focalization just slightly more clearly rendered. Knotting remains a juxtapositional and sequential strategy no matter how the page layout is broken down.

Schizo-Spatial Focalization

Let me then suggest a final idea about focalization as it relates to Kabuki's mental state. While focalization knots may occur in many different forms, what *Kabuki* does is to render focalization ambiguous and potentially unreliable. We are often not entirely sure if the information we are presented with is accurate or is some form of hallucination or dream that Kabuki experiences. Throughout *Skin Deep* there are several suggestions that Akemi is a figment of Kabuki's imagination rather than an actual person. In *Metamorphosis* we encounter so many different Noh agents in the Control Corps facility, all of whom suffer from various personality disorders, that we must wonder if Kabuki also suffers from a similar disorder. Since all the Noh agents suffer from identity issues, having either too many or too few identities, we cannot help but wonder if Kabuki projects these different characters.

I will term this aspect of focalization "schizo-spatial focalization." It is an intensification of focalization knots in which multiple spatial positions are rendered on the same page. The notion of spatial positioning in comics is complicated. Silke Horstkotte and Nancy Pedri argue that we should be careful not to conflate focalization with an optical position.[18] Similarly, Kukkonen insists that "the origin of the perspective of the image, that is, the spatial point from which it is perceived, is not marked."[19] Instead, we are more likely to understand focalization as being tied to who we see in the panel, rather than from what position the observer sees the figures in the panel.[20] The observer position is often complicated and not readily available, whether in narrative terms or in human embodiment terms (i.e., can we imagine being in such a physical position?). Graphic style, as has been noted, also participates in the rendering of focalization. With schizo-spatial focalization, I instead want to name instances where we have the same focalizer positioned in different spatial positions at the same time. While this is clearly not mimetically possible for us, it is spatially possible to produce such renderings in comics.

The opening pages (242–45) of *Metamorphosis* part 6 are three double splash pages that conclude in a single splash page and render visible Kabuki's complete mental breakdown. After these opening pages, the style changes dramatically and becomes far more coherent, and a conversation between Kabuki and the doctor takes over. These opening splash pages all have multiple characters drawn in distorted lines, with speech bubbles filled with nonsense and the emergence of Kabuki's narration. The characters may be inmates at the Control Corps facility, along with orderlies and guards, although some of them are memories; it is hard to make out which are which. The splash pages come off as incredibly messy and disorganized, with no clear reading progression and background writings that blur into each other, unreadable overall. Page 245 is slightly more organized, its left side dominated by small squares with small drawings of girls. The squares are not panels, and crayon drawings of Akemi's face, often rendered in childish lines or reduced to iconic representation, cross many of the squares. A relatively well-defined figure rests in the middle bottom, drawing or writing in a journal. Words are scrawled all over the page, following various winding lines and chaotic patterns. Five captions provide narration that serves as some form of narrative progression—Kabuki again encounters the doctor, who is busy looking in her Akemi ledger, attempting to understand Akemi. Much of the writing scrawled across the page seems to be from the doctor's journal, although the handwriting changes and the words are all jumbled; these words undoubtedly do not come directly from the doctor's journal.

There are two aspects of focalization at work here: knowledge and spatial position. The knowledge is marked as Kabuki's, even though most of the knowledge is scrambled, confused, and hard to decipher. As is so often the case in *Kabuki*, this focalization is expressed graphically, in the graphic style of the handwriting and also in the spatial scrawl of the writing all over the page. The writhing writing forces the reader to twist and turn the comic, and it also breaks the reading flow and direction. The story information—which in this case is mostly character information—is thus overlaid with Kabuki's mental state, that of a near breakdown. While there is no explicit reason to doubt what we are told, two pages later Kabuki realizes that a reflection in a door window is not Akemi but herself. Adding to this unreliability, the other inmates do not recognize Kabuki as she is pushed past them in a wheelchair.

This brings us to spatial positioning, which is entirely distorted on this page. On a splash page without any panels, the spatial perspective should be singular, restricted to just one observer. Yet that is not so. All the little figures are drawn in a child-like style, with a frontal perspective and no significant horizontal angle. The various renditions of Akemi's face are also all straight on but are angled around their own axes, several of them upside down or otherwise askew. As already noted, the writing is scrawled all over the page, some of it horizontally, some snaking in a bending line, and some upside down. The only figure that we can conceivably recognize as a character who is part of the action rather than added nondiegetically to the page is the doctor. Depicted as a sketch in faded pencil lines, she fades into the background but is drawn from a position above her, looking down on her writing in her journal. Some of the writing literally flows from her journal, though not the majority of it.

This page is a mess. This statement should not be understood as a criticism of Mack's style or his skill with page breakdowns. Everything here is intentionally designed to suggest the experience of a near breakdown: the elements are disorienting, confusing, incoherent. Even the spatial positioning of the reader experiences distortion, which occurs in two ways: graphically and materially. On the graphic level, everything about the drawing style, the layout, and the perspective is confusing. The spatial positioning cannot literally be above the doctor, since Kabuki is in a wheelchair. Yet, this is also not an instance of the character in the panel being the focalizer, since this page, like the ones preceding it, unequivocally belongs to Kabuki. In this way, spatial positioning and focalization run counter to each other and produce disorienting spatial relations. The same goes for the drawings of the children and Akemi. Although they are overlaid on the same page as the sketch of the doctor, the spatial positioning is not the same; the angles simply do not match. Yet again, this produces a spatially disorienting effect.

That brings us to the material level of spatial disorientation. As already noted, the writing from the doctor's journal is scrawled all over the page in a winding, disorganized pattern. If one wants to read all of the writing, there are two choices: strain to read writing that is on the side or upside down, or turn the book. Having to physically turn the book you are reading so that you can view it from various angles is unusual for comics, though not unheard of. *Kabuki* has a general tendency to feature angled writing, not just in *Metamorphosis* but also earlier (and later). In any case, having to physically turn the book in our hands is a nontrivial effort that breaks conventional reading flow.[21] What is more important in this case is that spatial positioning is literally changed for the reader. The object that we are actively looking at (even though this activity is mostly trivial and unmarked) suddenly requires nontrivial effort, and our unmarked spatial position is suddenly marked. The spatial positioning that is built into every image is disrupted here and becomes part of the experience of reading *Kabuki*.

My interest here is not to place Mack's artistic style within the tradition of Western visual art that disrupts perspective and spatial positioning, although it is evident from Mack's work on *Kabuki* and *Daredevil* that he is highly aware of this tradition and explicitly draws on it in many of his works. My argument here is limited to the spatial positioning within the comics page. By confronting readers with their own spatial positioning and forcing the reader to alter this position, *Kabuki* produces a disorienting experience that is confusing and lacks coherence. There are multiple spatial positions across this one splash page, and organizing that space into a coherent whole is difficult. In this way, the spatial positions and layout in general render Kabuki's mental breakdown visible through graphic style. Space becomes an expression of Kabuki's mental state.

This is schizo-spatial focalization: multiple spatial positions within one page, which is not divided into distinct panels, and all originating from the same focalizer at the same time. Schizo-spatial focalization is highly confusing and requires careful attention to parse the different levels of focalization. Various degrees of story, character, and world knowledge are (dis)arranged on the page, generating a jumble of information. While Kabuki is clearly undergoing some form of mental distress, it is crucial to note that I do not employ the term "schizo-spatial" as indicative of mental illness. I do not suggest that Mack's graphic style or spatial layout in any way represents the diagnosis of schizophrenia. What schizo-spatial focalization is meant to invoke is two things. First is the Greek root of the word meaning "to split," and the second is the production of realities that Gilles Deleuze and Félix Guattari associate with schizophrenia.[22] For Deleuze and Guattari, the figure of the schizophrenic is the one who invents realities beyond any limits and in so doing splits the world.

Schizo-spatial focalization is a spatial form that describes juxtaposed levels of information that cannot physically exist in reality but can exist on the comics page. Different spatial permutations produce novel ways of expressing knowledge while also expressing the subjectivity of the character. Spatial form becomes not simply a matter of nondiegetic gridding that organizes narrative events and information into a coherent flow but instead a part of the characters' experience—not just what they relate to us but how it feels to them. While all forms of spatial layouts necessarily participate in the reading experience, schizo-spatial layout describes the instances in which the layout is a spatial rendering of a character's subjective experience. In other words, as Deleuze and Guattari phrase it, "there is no need to distinguish here between producing and its product."[23] The spatial layout and the subjective experience of the focalizer are the same; it can only be expressed this way.

Consider page 172 of *Metamorphosis*, another splash page. Its primary spatial design is that of a maze seen from above. We can argue that the maze functions as one panel and that the bottom-right corner, although connected to the maze, is a separate panel. The smaller cartoon images may also be considered as separate panels. This bottom-right panel has Kabuki sitting on a toilet, while the maze has two cartoonish renderings of Kabuki and Akemi. In the top-left corner of the page is the beginning of the maze—a big red *X* that marks the spot with writing stating, "We are here," and a line drawing of Akemi's face. On the top right, outside of the maze, is written "minimum security," and on the bottom left, also outside of the maze, is the word "maximum," mirrored, with multiple instances of the word "security" scattered on the floor as if dropped. There is no dialogue per se, although there is a caption on the bottom right. This caption gives us information that the page itself does not ("someone is waiting for us") and propels us to the next page, where that someone is revealed.

The maze has writing in it, and this is what serves as the primary narration on this page. The story is that Akemi is trying to get Kabuki out of Control Corps. The writing that winds its way through the maze is Akemi relating the plan to Kabuki. In this way, the writing serves as a form of stand-in for Akemi and Kabuki making their way through the Control Corps facility—first past maximum security, through the air vents into minimum security, and then into a bathroom. The middle of the maze has a rendering of the blueprints, indicating the air vents that Kabuki and Akemi traverse, and then finally the maze leads to Kabuki on the toilet.

The spatial design of this page *is* the focalization. While there is verbal narration, the most expressive part of the page is the visual rendition of Kabuki and Akemi's escape. The page's spatial design is both the producer and the product of the narrative events. This focalization works through a literal-material expression. As readers, we have to twist and turn the book to read the narration, which is the reading equivalent of Kabuki and Akemi's escape. Although this page is a rare manifestation of comics' materiality and focalization as a function of that materiality and spatial design, it is simply one extreme of the permutations that page design may feature. Ian Hague has discussed this material aspect of twisting and turning the page as *directed touch*, where the reader interacts with the material object of the comic.[24] The scrawling and crawling lettering often used in *Kabuki* occurs often enough that this directed touch is part of its spatial form.

Mack has a tendency to produce splash pages that have inferred or suggested paneling. This tendency familiarizes readers somewhat with the otherwise somewhat challenging designs that break convention at every turn. Although this schizo-spatial focalization is never exactly normalized, it does become more and more familiar across the full run of *Kabuki*. What these page layouts show is also the primacy of the spatial. Far beyond gridding, spatial form enables more potentials in terms of how to arrange narrative and non-narrative information. We find a similar approach to schizo-spatiality (although without the directed touch) in Matz and Luc Jacamon's *The Killer*, in which jagged panels that mismatch bodies and objects express the killer's mental state, such as on pages 93 and 196.

Coda: Perspective in Comics

Narration in *Kabuki* and comics in general is highly determined by the spatial design of panel, sequence, page, and series. Different graphic styles evoke different kinds of narrators and may indicate narrator shifts in ways that are otherwise unmarked. Narrator shifts are not unlike time shifts but with the significant difference that time does not necessarily pass between narrator shifts. This is one way in which the sequential nature of comics need not tie temporal progression to spatial change. Simultaneity can be expressed in this way, even if we as readers necessarily must read across the page in some way. The linear-tabular choreography that crisscrosses comics pages must then be understood as not solely temporal in nature; plenty of these relations are instead associated with the narrator and narration.

Narration must also be associated with graphiation—the graphic style utilized to render the narrator visible. Graphiation lies halfway between narration and focalization: who relates the information and what information is related. The entire spatial design of panel, sequence, and page simultaneously presents and obscures narrative information and determines how that narrative information is experienced. Stick figures versus photorealistic paintings do not convey narrative information in the same way, and these designs impact not just experience but the form of narrative information. This is why graphic style must be analyzed, not just on the level of its aesthetic expression but in terms of how graphic style impacts the entire comics assemblage and its spatial arrangement.

With spatial design being tied to narration, focalization is another significant issue tied to spatial form. Determining story, character, and world knowledge rather than who narrates, focalization is often tied to the spatial juxtaposition of narrative information on panel, sequence, and page. One unique aspect of comics' narrational techniques is that focalization can knot. Rather than express narrative and temporal progression, spatial juxtaposition may also express multiple points of view simultaneously, which is the form of knotting. Knotting occurs within the same panel or splash page; otherwise, it is an instance of narrator shift, since in those cases there is a discernible shift in sequence. Knotting, then, is a spatial multiplication of narrative information from different sources and levels of narrative knowledge. Although comics are read in sequence like novels, the linear-tabular choreography enables shifts between individual panels or nodes on the page and the entirety of the page.

This brings us to the concept of spatial positioning, which is distinct from narrator shifts, graphiation, and knotting focalization. Most typically, spatial positioning is not marked as significant in comics; rather than occupying the space of perspective, narrative information is most often regarded as being attached to the character in the panel. Much like for other visual media such as film and TV, narrative attachment and knowledge depend on who we see, not the position from which we see something. Yet of course such conventions may be complicated by the narration. Comics afford the juxtaposition of two distinct and separate perspectives within the same spatial field. Such complications generate a tension between these simultaneous and juxtaposed perspectives. For *Kabuki*, but certainly not necessarily for all comics, this tension manifests as schizo-spatial focalization. Rather than being an inherent feature of spatial positioning, schizo-spatial focalization participates in the thematic resonance of Kabuki's mental strain and breakdown.

Much of the discussion in this chapter has focused on single panels or splash pages. This has been necessary in order to focus my analysis on the intricate shifts that occur in *Kabuki* and the ways in which space works through juxtaposition within the same frame. Of course, there is more sequentiality in comics than what occurs between different panels on a given page. This interaction between linear and tabular relations holds much potential in terms of narrational inventiveness, and *Kabuki* realizes much of this potential in significant ways. The story flow can be complicated in many different ways within a single or double page. However, we have yet to delve into how flow works across pages and to discover what forms of rhythms are produced by *Kabuki*. This is the aim of the next chapter.

4
Rhythms

Flow, Loops, and Coherence

The narrative trajectory of *Kabuki* is relatively straightforward to outline: Kabuki, an assassin for the shadowy Noh agency, takes revenge on her mother's killer, is captured by the Noh agency and subjected to psychiatric evaluation, breaks out, and escapes to the United States, where she tells her story in five books. However, this brief summary is about as accurate as saying that Proust's *In Search of Lost Time* is about eating cookies—accurate but lacking the details and singularities that make the story what it is. To understand and explicate the details of Kabuki's story, we need to better understand the rhythm and rhythmic design in comics storytelling.

Rhythms and Spatial Arrangement

Rhythmic design, or what Thierry Groensteen calls the "rhythmic function," is oddly underdeveloped in comics studies. Groensteen is the primary scholar to have developed any terminology for comics' rhythms. His definition is clear: rhythm "is imposed on it [the comics text] by the succession of frames," and this succession both propels the story (by giving more information) and arrests the story (by withholding information) in what he terms a "progression/retention" maneuver.[1] His argument is intuitive, and he develops his ideas further in *Comics and Narration*, where he draws on music terminology to suggest smooth/accentuated and cadenced/syncopated as the primary patterns that rhythms may have. The crucial point, for Groensteen and for me, is that rhythm cannot determine the duration of panels, only "time intervals that are felt, through an impression that is built up in stages."[2] So, rhythms do not determine the exact duration of a panel (ten seconds or five hours, for instance) but do signal the pace of relations between panels. Fast/slow can therefore be added as another pattern that rhythms may establish.

Such an approach to rhythm is useful for explaining the back-and-forth shifts in narrative action, as well as the other possible patterns that rhythm affords. James Kochalka, a comics writer who theorizes comics in his 1999 book *The Horrible Truth about Comics*, suggests that "rhythm is the key" to how "the continuing transitions from panel to panel . . . fall into understandable patterns."[3] Rather than the typology of transitions that Scott McCloud has suggested and that I discussed earlier, the transitions between panels are spatial arrangements, not simply in terms of sequence but also in terms of layout and panel size, shape, and so forth.

Consider page 197 of *Circle of Blood*, where Kabuki breaks into Ryuichi Kai's complex. The page is broken down into top and bottom frameless panels that show Kai's goons doing a karaoke rendition of INXS's "Devil Inside": nine panels of surveillance TV screens showing Kabuki breaking in and one inserted panel of the karaoke album. So, there are two narrative actions occurring. The top and bottom panels progress the narrative action of Kai's goons drinking, dancing, and singing. Literally in the middle of that is the narrative action of Kabuki entering the complex and killing various guards.

This is an alternating rhythm—between goons singing and Kabuki killing. The rhythm emerges from the different use of panels for each narrative action. The top and bottom panels take up the width of the page and so prolong the singing and dancing. The surveillance TV panels are smaller and gridded to produce a staccato rhythm of more intense events: one guard shooting, Kabuki shooting that guard, that guard falling, the next guard moving in, Kabuki kicking him down, Kabuki facing the camera, and the camera lens shattering. The pace between the two different narrative actions is different—one feels continuous, the other chopped into smaller moments. The rhythm also alternates between these two different story lines.[4] Furthermore, the speech balloons of the goons' singing continue as captions in the panels of Kabuki breaking in. This has an anchoring function of making readers understand that these two narrative actions occur simultaneously.

Another rhythmic function underscores this simultaneity. The top and bottom panels have three speech bubbles each, whereas all but one of the surveillance TV panels have one caption. Spatially, the balloons and captions are on the same horizontal axis, suggesting that the duration across the top and bottom panels is similar to that of three of the surveillance TV panels. This is part of this page's rhythmic design and makes the page quite coherent, despite two challenges. First, the top panel is the first time we see the goons; they have not been introduced on previous pages, and so we need to read them into the overall rhythm of Kabuki entering the complex. Second, this is the first page that has surveillance TV panels, whereas on the previous pages we have followed Kabuki directly, not through a different narrator.[5] The rhythm of the vertical alignment is both an example of polyrhythm (two different rhythms that work in unison) and an example of a steady beat. While the contents of the nine surveillance TV panels suggest a much slower pace internal to each panel (what McCloud would call moment-to-moment pacing), the duration of the wider panels is far more fluid.

Groensteen's concept of rhythm works well, then, to explain what he calls the narrative's rhythmic beat.[6] From this idea, he goes on to explain the emphasis of repetition, alternation, and progressivity. We can quibble and argue that there should also be room for the pause—the inserted panel that does not fall in line with the cadence of the beat. In the page discussed above, that would be the inserted panel of the karaoke album. This panel serves little purpose (other than to signal to the reader that INXS is still listened to in future cyberpunk Japan) and does not match the rhythmic beat of the other panels. Its off-kilter position within the gridding underscores this fact as well. The idea of the pause panel is certainly related to that of the pillow panel but with one main exception. Where the pillow panel invites contemplation and exists mainly outside narrative flow, the pause panel is a pause in the narrative flow, not for contemplation but to suggest a shift or a difference in narrative pace.

Rhythm exists not only on a single page but across multiple pages, whether as part of a single scene, a segment, an issue, or whichever narrative unit we wish to demarcate. In this instance, the narrative unit that makes the most sense is that of act 5 of *Circle of Blood*. This issue opens with Kabuki descending on Kai's complex and ends with Kabuki and Kai facing off. In narrative terms, we have both a clear beginning and a clear ending that leads directly to a cliffhanger, carrying readers forward to the next issue. The rhythms of this issue certainly exhibit repetition, alternation, and progressivity. But there is one major aspect that Groensteen has left out, and that is rhythmic emphasis. While narrative events may repeat and alternate, as in the example above, and also progress either quickly or slowly, some narrative events are given more emphasis than others.

There are two main strategies for rhythmic emphasis. Both are spatial. The first is a matter of page layout, so that the last panel on the page has a cliffhanger that propels the narrative further and the reader to the next page. There are two versions of this—left-hand pages, where the reader must simply glance to the top of the next page, and right-hand pages, where the reader must turn the page to see what happens. The right-hand page's last panel is therefore often the most suspenseful, since this placement obscures the outcome of the event, urging the reader to turn the page. This form of arrangement is also a way for the linear-tabular interaction to postpone outcomes and so produce curiosity.

The other strategy is less a matter of page layout sequentiality and more a matter of panel size. A larger panel size, relative to the other panels around it, speaks to intensified significance, whether narrative or not. There is no hard-and-fast rule about duration here, nor does the larger panel necessarily carry the most narrative information. My argument is simply that larger panels generate emphasis as a function of the spatial emphasis. The panel may contain an imposing tableau, a shocking reveal, or something else. What matters is that a larger panel alters reading flow and often makes readers pay more attention. Although that stretches reading duration, these later panels are not instances of pauses, since they carry more significance. In other words, we should be working with three forms of rhythmic markers—not just the beat but pause, beat, and emphasis.

As an example, consider page 196 of *Circle of Blood*, the preceding page to the example above. This page has four panels, technically all inserted on a white-and-black background with patterned corners. The first three panels get increasingly smaller, while the fourth panel takes up three-quarters of the page. But the dominant panel does not contain any urgent narrative action, does not repeat or alternate narrative actions, and moves narrative progress only slightly. Yet, it is by far the more dramatic panel, urging us to marvel at Kabuki in full display.

Emphasis also impacts narrative pacing. The first three panels are small and easily perceived. The narrative action is clear and well articulated. The narrative flow is almost at scanning speed, fully propelling the reader forward in the narrative. The fourth panel makes the reader slow down and take in the imposing, almost threatening panel of Kabuki. Pacing slows down not due to the volume of detail but simply so that the reader is able to take in the art and its design. In terms of the linear-tabular relations, the reader's eyes are drawn to the fourth panel first before reading direction reverts to the first three panels, with full awareness of Kabuki's actions. In other words, the fourth panel and its size make the reader skip ahead, essentially involuntarily, and thus one reads the earlier panels while already knowing what will happen afterward. This page's layout is therefore less about tension and suspense—the fourth panel does not have any cliffhanger function to propel the reader to the next page—but instead serves to underline Kabuki's lethal nature.

If one looks at the full run of act 5, it becomes clear that there is no standard gridding that continues for more than two or three pages. Most pages have singular layouts that do not repeat on the next page. There is no waffle-iron technique here, and this goes for most of the entire *Kabuki* series run; even at his most conventional in *Fear the Reaper*, the first *Kabuki* publication, David Mack continuously varies layouts and patterns. Lack of a regular rhythm means that most narrative trajectories have some form of accentuated rhythm instead. Since even this accentuation changes, the rhythms vary from pensive to staccato. For act 5, the rhythm alternates between emphatic panels and beat panels, interspersed with some pauses. The emphatic panels are of Kabuki flying through the

9. *Kabuki: Circle of Blood*, 196.

rain, walking down stairs, diving into water. These panels of movement have an ambiguous, extended duration that often recapitulates or concludes a much longer duration or narrative action. This is part of their emphatic extending of duration—we are invited to imagine the events in between, in a process not unlike McCloud's notion of closure. With the beat panels, the sequential structure is different. These panels display short, sharp moments of Kabuki killing people, showing one action per panel: shooting a gun, kicking a face, falling down, and so on. The effect is one of suspenseful intensity, appropriate for what is essentially an action-thriller comic.

The major shift in rhythm comes about a third of the way through the issue, when Kabuki faces Kai. The page that reveals Kai's presence (page 200) has several inserted panels on a dominant panel that shows Kabuki entering a room, with a small inserted panel, in the bottom-right corner, featuring Kai. This produces the cliffhanger effect of compelling the reader to turn to the next page. The next three pages are double splash pages, the first two showing a chaotic flurry of letters and panels all atumble over the page, at all kinds of angles. We can also see that the panels on the second double splash page are less chaotic than the first, and on the third splash page there is a full image, and we recognize that the earlier, jumbled panels were fragments of this page. With the upside-down panels, letters that belong to nowhere, and so on, this is an early instance of schizo-spatial focalization in *Kabuki*, and unlike in the later collections, the fragmentation is quickly recovered. Rhythmically, these three double splash pages prolong the reading of the page, slowing the narrative flow. The fast-paced narrative unfolding of the earlier pages stops in its tracks, and a relatively simple overview page, presenting the characters in a room and their reaction to Kabuki's entrance, is instead stretched over three double pages.

This prolonging effect shows an important aspect of rhythm that Groensteen only briefly mentions and then passes over for the rest of his discussion: rhythm is "never a matter of time intervals that can be measured but of time intervals that are felt."[7] My interest here is not in returning to a discussion of time shifts between panels. Instead, what is important about Groensteen's argument about rhythm is that it is *felt*, not measured. To say that rhythm is felt and not measured does not mean that it cannot be analyzed. It means that there is no fixed meter or pattern to which comics must conform. Instead, any rhythmic pattern may be used to express narrative events and action. Narrative rhythms participate in what makes the story feel hectic, placid, smooth, or any number of different experiences.

Narrative Flow

Groensteen mounts a defense of the regular rhythm of the grid. Although there is no need to summarize his arguments, it should be clear that regular gridding allows for a highly stable, well-articulated rhythmic flow. Reading progression is clearly organized, the narrative's progressivity has a well-defined cadence, and the experience is smooth. There is an overlap between what I termed the flow of time in chapter 2 and the idea of narrative flow that I develop here. To a certain extent, they are identical, in that narrative flow expresses a flow of time in its narrative progressivity. Action after action, event after event, produces a temporal flow as well as a narrative flow. However, what I am focusing on here is the regular rhythm that leads to an experience of narrative flow.

There are plenty of instances of narrative flow in *Kabuki*. Even if regular rhythms are rarely dominant in the series, most of the collections have narrative flow. A regular rhythm is not the only way to achieve narrative flow, as long as the various shifts between panels are clearly articulated, whether it is a matter of time shifts, narrator shifts, or something else. The spatial layout plays a huge role in this redirect. So to illustrate how narrative flow works despite a lack of regular rhythm, consider the pages (220 and 221) that open act 6 of *Circle of Blood*. This is the opening of the face-off between Kabuki and Kai. The two pages are mostly mirrors of each other, with three smaller panels to the right and the left of the main ones, respectively. The smaller panels are filled with rows of *s*'s, *k*'s, and *h*'s, rendering a whistling type of sound. On page 220 the creators and editors for this issue are listed in the small panels, while on page 221 Kabuki's iconic face mask is rendered across all three smaller panels.

Page 220 has one large, dominant panel of Kabuki dying on her mother's grave, with her mother's face at the top of the panel—a repetition of page 93. Page 221 has three panels that show the carnage that Kabuki has wreaked on Kai's guards. The lyrics to Velvet Underground's "Femme Fatale" are written across the page. The gridding in these two pages is not regular, in the sense of following the same panel layout. The pages are similar enough, however, that the narrative information is clearly articulated. Narrative flow is achieved, despite the rather abrupt shifts in time. The dominant panel on page 220 is disconnected from the narrative setup but important for thematic purposes and is a central motif of the series. The three main panels on page 221 are essentially pause panels—there is little narrative action, but they help to provide context and mood. The temporal shift is intelligible, the shifts between different places of the same location are legible. There is smooth narrative flow that expresses narrative action clearly.

The disruption comes with page 222—a double splash page with several panels, all of them at canted angles. The narrative action is the fight between Kabuki and Kai, but the spatial layout is not smooth and does not facilitate narrative flow. The left-hand side has the largest panel, tilted at a 45-degree angle. The progression from the earlier page is maintained by having the dead guard from the last panel in the background of this panel. Kabuki and Kai are in front, hurtling toward each other. Yet even the composition within the panel is askew, with the guard and the floor at an angle that does not match the angle of the panel. The right-hand side has five panels of punches thrown, the panels themselves distorted trapezoids and the angles of composition canted in all of them. There are musical note icons, graphic onomatopoeia from fighting, the title (*Circle of Blood: Final Curtain*), song lyrics, and various embellishments.

All in all, the impression is a visual jumble, hectic without a clear narrative progression. The right-hand side of the double page has a higher degree of narrative flow, as the panels are placed below each other and signal a clear shifting between them. The immediate impression is one of confusion, an impression that replicates the hectic fight between Kabuki and Kai, and this confusion slows the reading flow. Readers can no longer easily move through panels and panel shifts but instead have to orient themselves more deliberately within the double splash page. Once that has happened, however, narrative progression returns and the narrative flow resumes. Much like the explosion of panels in act 5, what happens on this splash page is mostly a pause-emphasis reaction that delays the narrative beat panels until orientation is reestablished. The canted angles of both panels and compositions within panels participate in intensifying the confusion. However, the splash page is not so disorganized that flow breaks down completely. Narrative movement is retained after a brief pause.

This is an example of how spatial layouts impact the narrative rhythm. While gridding enables a well-defined rhythm, turbulence can be introduced by disrupting such regular gridding and not following any form of regular gridding across several pages. Although the story does not become incomprehensible or that much harder to follow, reading duration is prolonged and the tension between narrative duration and reading duration is intensified. The page layout works as a kind of emphasis by prolonging reading duration. Although this prolonging is not measurable as such, we must assume that the fight between Kabuki and Kai is hectic and that each panel would last only a few seconds. But due to the jumbled panel flow, the reading duration is necessarily longer. Prolonging this duration adds emphasis, simply because we stay with the fight longer.

The turbulent flow in this example is relatively easily navigated. This ease is furthered by the fact that a more regular gridding returns on the next page. There is no waffle-iron gridding in *Circle of Blood* or any of the other collections—there are stretches of pages that contain the same or similar breakdowns, but the rhythms remain accentuated and vary often. The earlier collections (*Fear the Reaper* and *Circle of Blood*, as well as *Masks of the Noh*, even though it is a spin-off) are generally marked by varied but mostly regular breakdowns with only brief deviations, such as the above example. The further along in the saga we go, the more expressive the breakdowns get (the same is true for *Dreams*).

Narrative Turbulence

Turbulent rhythms begin to take over in *Metamorphosis*, where the choreography between panels becomes increasingly accentuated. *Metamorphosis* moves toward a reliance on splash pages, so much so that most of the story unfolds across splash pages, rather than the far more conventional panel progressions. Act 5 of *Metamorphosis* is a good example of how these splash pages produce turbulent rhythm shifts that propel the narrative, although not in a smooth manner.

First of all, each of the splash pages in act 5 of *Metamorphosis* is highly individualized so that there are few direct connections between them, whether graphically, spatially, or narratively. On the level of story, the entire act is taken up by Kabuki attacking Control Corps guards in order to break free; the act finishes with her being overpowered and falling unconscious. But on the level of plot, everything is far more complicated. The title page is a double splash page, as are the next four spreads (eight pages). The opening splash page shows Kabuki's upper body, with the lower part of her face visible. Then there follow two double splash pages on black background, full bleed. The first of these has captions written in angled text, with words changing sizes at random, guards placed willy-nilly on the page, while the bottom-right corner has a panel of Kabuki's face in inverted color. The next double splash page has Kabuki's face in an inserted panel, as well as several panels of a guard attacking Kabuki, Kabuki kicking him in a repeated panel, and his face in pain. The panels are jumbled, with no linear progression between them—it is as if the guard's face in pain comes before Kabuki kicks him. The panels feel more like still moments, or snapshots of something that is happening, but we do not have full access to the action.

The same rhythm emerges from the next two double splash pages with white backgrounds. Several inserted panels, often overlapping split panels, portray guards who look alike, with Kabuki kicking and fighting in close-ups and smaller panels. The lack of similar layouts, clear reading flow, and still panels produces a jagged rhythm that is confusing. A panel in the upper-right corner has causality flowing down and left, while another panel sequence flows down and right. And yet all these panels show movements that have been laid out in the first panel, an intricate pattern of Kabuki's (expected?) movements between all the guards. Panels alternate in size, a huge panel dominates the last double splash page of Kabuki's kicking someone, and nine much smaller panels show individual moments of the fight. And on the right side, Kabuki fighting a guard transitions into the shape of a kanji, leaving the rest of the page white.

And then comes a full-page splash entirely in white with kanjis drawn on it and Kabuki, with four arms, in a majestic leap. The four arms clearly suggest Kabuki's speed, but the effect after the preceding jumbled and chaotic pages is one of calm and stillness, not speed. Kabuki fights, the kanjis turn into note annotations, and Kabuki morphs into a string of notes coming from the general's piano. Another full splash page shows Kabuki as a ballet dancer, with a musical score angling around the page, even across Kabuki's body. Kabuki as a child, learning music, the general playing piano, Kabuki dancing in a ball gown with a man in a tuxedo, now in many smaller panels—this flashback sequence functions ambiguously: the dance is at times presented as if the two dancers are actually fighting, rather than dancing. Yet, because the figures are only in silhouette, it is hard to tell.

This forms a turbulent rhythm, where the fighting blends with the flashback and marks the moments differently. This is not an alternating rhythm, since there are not two story lines that take turns. Instead, the one story line informs the other, shifting between different depths of Kabuki's subjectivity: the present of the fight, the pasts of her as a child and young adult, her time with Akemi. This blurring of different events from different times produces a turbulent rhythm in which the present and pasts inform each other. This relationship is accentuated and nonlinear and does not produce narrative progressivity. The relationship between fighting to escape Control Corps and

Kabuki's past is not narratively motivated and has no bearing on the narrative events as such. Instead, these events are motivated by Kabuki reflecting on why she ever ended up as an assassin. We can also argue that the relation is spatially motivated, in the way that dancing and fighting resemble each other. The movements of bodies and stances are all similar enough that the transitions between present and pasts produce easy visual flow. It is the narrative flow that is complex; even the captions that anchor that narrative flow do not fully explain these shifts.

Another instance of turbulent rhythm emerges between pages 231 and 232. After a long series of splash pages, 231 almost explodes with panels: eighteen panels in an almost four-horizontal, five-vertical grid, with a few of the unaligned panels shifting erratically between fighting, dancing, and the general playing piano. This turbulent rhythm intensifies the relation between these different pasts and the present. The turbulent rhythm carries over to the next page, which has a similar panel rhythm. Page 232 has seventeen panels in what starts out as a four-horizontal, five-vertical grid, with the first panel unaligned. Unlike the previous page, the last three panels drop out of the grid alignment, suggesting a fall or tapering off. Every panel is a rendition of Akemi in varying graphic styles, from Mack's baseline style, watercolor, and Post-it notes to photorealism, Japanese collage, cubism, surrealism, and more. The disruptive shift between the two pages is lessened by having a similar panel rhythm, yet this remains a syncopated rhythm. There are no time shifts indicated here, only an intensification of Akemi's significance for Kabuki.

And just like that, the splash pages return and Kabuki has a few moments of respite before more guards descend. As Kabuki is knocked unconscious, the issue ends. It ends with another splash page, which shows the guards in pencil outline, small in the background, with Siamese large in the foreground, looking at the reader and saying "shhhh." Although an arresting final page, which also serves as a cliffhanger to propel us to the next issue, it is also narratively confusing. Siamese are not part of this story line, they are not present in the Control Corps facility to our knowledge, and they do not serve as narrators. Their presence remains a mystery. And yet there is a convoluted rhythmic logic to their presence, which brings up the idea of narrative rhythmic loops.

Narrative Loops

As we may remember, *Skin Deep* opened with Siamese breaking into the Control Corps facility, finding Kabuki dead, and blowing up her corpse. A temporal shift indicated that this was a flashback, something that had happened prior to Kabuki being interviewed by the Control Corps doctor. At the end of *Skin Deep*, there is a suggestion that it was actually a flashforward. Toward the end of *Metamorphosis*, in act 8 out of nine acts total, we suddenly find the exact same panels and pages from *Skin Deep* but with some of the alternate panels being removed. This sequence has the appearance of being inserted into the pages of *Metamorphosis*—they are slightly smaller than the original page layouts, having wider borders. There is also a notable shift in graphic style, from the more jagged, rougher, and watercolor-dominated style of late *Metamorphosis* to the somewhat smoother lines and paint of early *Skin Deep*. Speaking from narrative progression, the page prior to the inserts has the doctor walking off the bottom panel. After the Siamese insert, we have the doctor walking through the rain, but on the next page we see that it is Kabuki dressed as the doctor.

Although this event is a strong narrative twist, that is not my focus here. Instead, many different bits of plot repeat across the *Kabuki* collections, sometimes from different character perspectives. While loops are typically associated with time, the loops that I investigate here once again are related to spatial form. There are two kinds of looping at work in *Kabuki*. The most prominent one is that of the repeated or restated panel, something that I have already discussed at length in various ways. However, the repeated pages of the Siamese insert warrant further discussion. The other looping form is connected to focalization, where some events are repeated from a different character's perspective. In the case of Scarab, this change in character perspective actually revises and expands on earlier versions of events. In both cases, of course, the loop form significantly revises narrative events that have already been presented.

In the first loop form that restates events, the narrative revision alters the rhythm that previously existed in *Skin Deep*. As the plot loops back and alters the sequence of events, it produces a turbulent rhythm that reflects backward on the construction of story and necessitates a revision. This is a spatial rearrangement of the sequence of narrative events. On the level of plot, the restating falls into a new, different sequence. Restating the same events changes their meaning, simply because they are now part of a different sequence. Such changes have affinities with "retcon" (retroactive continuity), a device typical in many long-running serial comics, where characters' origins, story, or world are changed to fit a new continuity.[8] The forward loop in *Kabuki* is of a limited nature, what Andrew Friedenthal calls a reinterpretation, which is where the narrative is revealed to have always already been this way, even though readers had not been made aware.[9] This restating loop may be contrasted with the refrain that I discussed in chapter 1. The refrain deemphasizes narrative change in favor of sameness, while the loop form here revises the narrative construction of the story.

The restated panels of Siamese are changed in two ways. The first is their placement within the narrative sequence, which is articulated by their framing. The other is that the first instance of these pages had alternating panels, interspersed with panels of distortion that alternated between Kabuki's story line and Siamese breaking in. This had signaled a flashback sequence of Kabuki's memory of this event, but it is instead a loop forward rather than a loop backward.

This forward loop is what alters the level of story. If one considers the story's actual chronological sequence, the repeated-but-revised panels are actually the original occurrence of the events depicted, rather than flashbacks to earlier events. In this way, a paradoxical rhythm troubles the level of plot and story. From a temporal perspective, time is looped around and revised. What is more important is that, considered from plot to story line, causality shifts around and so events now have a different sequence. Spatial form informs time, not the other way around. What this means is that causality is spatial in comics, rather than temporal. As time emerges from the spatial shifts in sequence, so causality emerges as the rhythm of that temporal expression. In this instance, what we find is that the obfuscated nonlinear sequence of Siamese breaking in and locating Kabuki produces what we might term a narrative arrhythmia. Causality breaks down and must be rearranged. Plot loops occur when coherence breaks down and the narrative sequence must be revised. These are moments of incoherence, in which the narrative does not flow. Instead, we find a turbulent narrative rhythm that not only surprises and shocks us but also emphasizes narrative unreliability.

That brings us to the other loop form—focalization. This loop form occurs several times across different collections. The crucial moment is that the doctor who had been having treatment sessions with Kabuki has been killed and a Noh agent has taken her place. Who this Noh agent might be is unknown in the first loop of the story line. This twist occurs in *Metamorphosis* right before the section with Siamese breaking into the Control Corps facility. Pages 288 and 289, which conclude act 7, are especially significant. Act 8 opens with a recap, restating the reveal that a Noh agent (identity still unknown) confronts Kabuki. The narration then explicitly states, "Cut. Stop. Rewind," and literally skips back. A sequence of highly abstract pages depicts the confrontation and fight against the Noh agent, whose identity is not revealed here, as each page shows a different agent. Kabuki kills the Noh agent, after which the narrative sequence skips to Siamese breaking in and finding Kabuki. This event is now revised, and we know that the body is not Kabuki but the other Noh agent. After the explosion, the story returns to the present moment, with Kabuki dressed as the doctor and leaving Control Corps.

Most of act 8 is a reflexive moment that revises time, as noted above. It also shows Kabuki's blurry perception of reality. What I am most interested in here, however, is something that does not happen just here in *Metamorphosis* but connects with the spin-off collection *Scarab: Lost in Translation*. In the first spin-off collection, *Masks of the Noh*, all the different Noh agents are illustrated by different artists. The limited appearance of Kabuki in that collection is illustrated by David Mack. Scarab is illustrated by Rick Mays and is the main character of *Masks of the Noh*, having two chapters rather than one, like most of the other agents. With *Scarab: Lost in Translation*, Mack and Mays continue their collaboration on Scarab's story. Mays's style takes on an even stronger manga-cartoonish look, and most of the story maintains the feel of a manga love story. The end, however, connects directly to the encounter between Kabuki and the unknown Noh agent. Within the frame of Scarab's story, most of the narrative focuses on Scarab's early life—her origin story, her role in Noh TV, and her love affair with a man named Yukio. At the end of *Scarab: Lost in Translation*, Scarab is going to run away with Yukio but has one final job left.

This job is of course to locate and kill Kabuki. The narration in *Scarab: Lost in Translation* alternates between Scarab's actual life and the depiction on the Noh TV animated series of the agents' exploits. Scarab relates that in the animated version of the Noh agents' life, they do not encounter the real Kabuki but an evil version of her. The agents then stop the evil version, bring the real Kabuki back, and everything is resolved with a happy ending. That is not what actually happens, as Scarab gets ready and goes to confront Kabuki. We see Scarab dress as the doctor, still in Mays's soft, clear lines, each page shifting to a full page of the Noh agents fighting each other in the animated show. This is when we learn that the unknown agent who posed as the doctor in *Metamorphosis* is/was actually Scarab.

As Scarab encounters Kabuki, however, the graphic style shifts and we see Mack's rendition of the encounter from *Metamorphosis*. The page layout and graphic style are copied from *Metamorphosis*; all that has been changed is that the caption narration attached to Scarab instead of Kabuki is typed, not handwritten. The shift in style is dramatic, Mack's and Mays's styles having little in common even though both feature only black and white.

The next page shifts back to a splash page of Noh agents fighting in the animated series and then back to Mack drawing a page from Scarab's perspective but borrowing panel compositions from *Metamorphosis*. Almost identical except for the shift to black-and-white line drawing contrasted to the full-color paintings in *Metamorphosis*, this page layout has been altered by Mack so as to restrict focalization to Scarab's plane. It also brings in panels from the next page in *Metamorphosis* to this same page in *Scarab: Lost in Translation*. Then it's back to a splash page of Mays's that depicts the animated show's version of Scarab and Kabuki's fight. Following that is a new page where panels appear to alternate between Mays's and Mack's

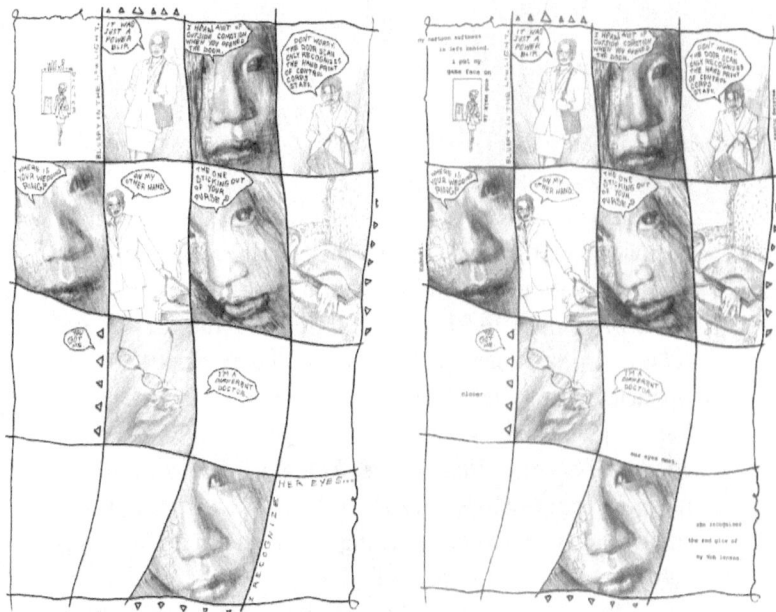

10. *Kabuki: Metamorphosis*, 288, and *Scarab: Lost in Translation*, 320.

illustrations, with panel borders that are wavy like the ones from Mack and the drawing style quite distinct between each panel. The panels done by Mack emulate but do not restate panels from *Metamorphosis*—a knife in a hand, a face whispering "out" are present in both but done slightly differently, unlike the restating of the two earlier pages.

Scarab dies. Yukio goes to the place where they agreed to meet prior to running away and waits alone. *Scarab: Lost in Translation* ends. And so does this complex narrative rhythm that articulates across two collections and shifts subtly between two distinct levels of focalization, even though some panels and pages are restated. This loop form repeats story events almost beat by beat, but by shifting the level of focalization to a different character, the rhythm does become different as panels shift ever so slightly. More markedly, in *Scarab: Lost in Translation* the narrative rhythm also shifts due to the alternating rhythm

RHYTHMS 143

of the Scarab story line and animated television series story line. Suddenly, there is far more character backstory to Scarab, and the mood of the event changes.

The mood in *Metamorphosis* is highly confused and unstable because of Kabuki's state of mind, yet her fight against Scarab is also liberating. Kabuki manages to escape Control Corps and is on her way to freedom. This opens up the subsequent collection, *The Alchemy*, to fully explore and conclude Kabuki's character arc; the fight against Scarab, brutal as it is, is positive. Kabuki expands and grows, and she becomes someone else, as is signaled by the collection's title. Yet Scarab's development has the exact opposite trajectory. Here, the story ends with a tragedy, the loneliness of Yukio calling her name and the last page completely black with two small white birds on the bottom left.

This loop form revises not just the temporal sequence of these events but also their mood. The liberating mood at the end of *Metamorphosis* stands in stark contrast to the tragic mood of *Scarab: Lost in Translation*. No longer simply a liberating moment for Kabuki, her escaping the Control Corps facility is now also tinged with sadness for Scarab's death and the lost love between her and Yukio. More so than exploring the backstory of Scarab, *Scarab: Lost in Translation* loops back and forces a challenge to one character trajectory due to another character trajectory. The spatial rhythm that we find across these collections remains an instance of braiding but one pushed to an extreme due to the focalization shifts.

Essentially, the two narrative rhythms work against each other, each presenting a different character in different ways. Narrative loops do more than just restate known narrative information. Instead, they may add characterization and narrative revision, if not on the level of what happens, then at least on the level of narrative mood. While the main story line remains Kabuki's and is by far the longest, the spin-off does provide subtle elaborations of what happens around Kabuki. With most of the collections being so restricted to Kabuki's focalization, gaining different and broader narrative information becomes part of a more turbulent narrative rhythm. Narrative rhythms are challenged through this alteration of sequence, not just because the temporal-causal flow is revised but because mood is also revised.

Rhythmic Coherence

Rhythm's primary function is generally to produce a sense of unity or coherence. Rhythmic flow participates in generating coherence, while turbulent rhythms more often place coherence under pressure. I want to use the idea of rhythmic coherence here to explore Kabuki's character and identity. Kabuki/Ukiko is often under mental strain, and she undergoes a major transformation throughout the entire series. In the same vein, how is character change registered spatially? As for the rest of this chapter, spatial form is meant in relation to both the literal spatial layout of the page and the sequential spatiality of the narrative.

When the series opens with *Fear the Reaper* and *Circle of Blood*, Kabuki is a traumatized but ruthless assassin out for vengeance. She is competent, driven, and in many ways a formulaic action character. As is also typical for action comics characters, she has an elaborate backstory that provides her motivation. As the two first collections progress, we learn more and more about her and her mother's past. This produces an alternating rhythm in the present story line of Kabuki, the Noh agency, and her vengeance. This rhythm emerges slowly. *Fear the Reaper* has four scenes. The first three are focused entirely on Kabuki's hunt for Snow, a drug lord whom the Noh agency wants executed. When she encounters Snow, a little information about her past is given, but the fourth scene is entirely focused on Kabuki's past. This provides a progressive connection that is linear: A, A, A, B—one story line per scene. *Fear the Reaper* follows a clear rhythm that connects events into a progressive narrative trajectory. This spatial rhythm moves forward in time and builds story more than character, until the fourth scene, which alternates in time (present/past) to develop not Kabuki but Kabuki's mother. This may be the main deviation from an otherwise conventional rhythmic flow, and it produces a high degree of rhythmic coherence in relation to Kabuki.

This rhythmic coherence becomes more complicated in *Circle of Blood*. In its six acts, the story of Kabuki expands both forward and especially backward. The collection opens with Kabuki assassinating one of Ryuichi Kai's gang members, then progresses to a meeting of the circle of Noh, where the leader of the circle, known as only "the Devil," discusses how best to locate and kill Kai. We remain within the A story line, and Kabuki's arc progresses only in relation to the plot; the two trajectories are on the same plane and the same rhythm. After the meeting, Kabuki goes to her mother's grave, and the narrative shifts to explore Kai's relationship with the general and Kabuki's mother. We learn that Kai is Kabuki's father, because he had raped Tsukiko, and so the C story line of Kai meshes with Tsukiko's B story line, which in turn meshes with a D story line of Kabuki's birth and murder by Kai. Within in the first act, we end up back in the present with the Devil revealing himself to have been Kai all along. In terms of story lines, we have a rhythm of A, C, B, D—a more complex interweaving than the prologue yet one that helps establish coherence for Kabuki.

Although counting is not everything, we can get more detail out of the rhythmic coherence. Setting one page as one narrative beat, we find the following detailed pattern: A12, B1, C4, B5, C9, B3, D12, A3, where the number after each letter signals the number of pages spent on that character. The page counts provide a sense of how much plot time is spent on each story line, alongside a sense of the brief interspersing of different time lines. The story lines are interwoven and so should not be considered fully distinct, but what this rhythmic pattern reveals is that the majority of act 1 is set in the past (story lines B through D), and then at the end the narrative returns to the present day for the big reveal that the Devil is Kai. Looking at coherence, we can also see that constant shifts connect Kai, Tsukiko, and Kabuki. It is easy enough to regard this as the backstory for Kabuki in the vein of many superhero comics, and it seems natural that this is the convention that Mack emulates, deliberately or not.

So, despite the rather rapid-fire shifts in narrative time and character focus, several connections are made that generate coherence for Kabuki (and to a lesser extent for Tsukiko and Kai). As we learn more about Kabuki's backstory, we begin to better understand Kabuki and her motivations—she becomes a more fully fleshed out character. This is hardly novel or surprising. In many ways, this is the conventional narrative sequentiality—one panel, one sequence, one page after another all build narrative events that build the story. *Kabuki*'s use of a nonlinear structure, however, employs a form of rhythmic coherence that serves to connect certain panel designs with certain events and emotional attachments. These connections go beyond narrative sequentiality and instead connect distinct events.

One main connection concerns Kabuki's birth and death. After Kai's assault of Tsukiko, Kabuki is born. This is presented on a page with two panels—the dominant one of the doctor and nurse helping Kabuki into the world and the smaller panel, on page 88, that shows Kabuki's face. When Kai learns that Kabuki is his child, he meets her at Tsukiko's grave and attacks Kabuki. Page 94 shows Kabuki being resuscitated, with the doctor appearing similar to the one delivering her as a baby and the male nurse wearing glasses similar to those worn by the nurse in attendance at her birth. The page layout echoes the birth page, with one dominant panel of the doctor bringing Kabuki back to life and one smaller panel that restates the image of the doctor's hands on Kabuki's chest. In other words, a rhythm is endowed with two beats of similar panels. This connects the events in each panel with the other, instating a thematic of life, death, and rebirth that is articulated across several connections. In *Circle of Blood* this specific panel rhythm emerges only once (which is to say twice).

This is how coherence is established in a nonlinear manner—two different past events are connected with current events as flashbacks but also through spatial means. Not just the spatiality of narrative sequence but also spatial composition and graphic style participate in making these two events cohere, linking them thematically. A rhythmic character coherence emerges from the birth-death-rebirth rhythm, which is most clearly marked in the early collections of *Kabuki*. We find several beats that connect back and forth across the collections and across Kabuki's life and narrative. It is also where spatial rhymes connect with narrative rhythms.

A few pages after the resuscitation page, the panel of Kabuki holding her mask in her hands that ended *Fear the Reaper* is restated, first as a single panel on page 97 and then as a full page on page 98, where she lifts her mask to reveal her face. While not a surprise twist in the way that Kai being the Devil is a twist five pages later, this revelation does produce another thematic resonance of masks, secrets, and identities. The reveal concludes the origin story of Kabuki, and the alternating rhythm of Kabuki's arc and Kai's arc produces a parallelism that associates the two characters with each other, a coherence that is further underlined by iconic similarities such as a facial scar and a dragon tattoo.

This rhythm of birth-death-rebirth connects Tsukiko, Kai, and Kabuki across the different narrative trajectories and produces coherence within a nonlinear plot. Causality emerges from these nonlinear connections as a continuous story is formed. But this causality is more than simple linearity—it is the growing tragedy of Kabuki's life, which is necessarily understood in relation to this birth-death-rebirth coherence. I have already accounted for the linkage produced by the spatial rhymes in *Fear the Reaper* in chapter 1. Here we can see how spatial rhymes add coherence to the narrative rhythms, since it is the restating and rhyming of panels that facilitate this coherence. By making the pages and panels resemble each other, rather than diverge, Mack makes the associations tighter, the events more closely connected.

There are two ways that we can see this. The first is closeness, measured in pages. All of Kabuki's childhood and early years are condensed into a few pages, making her birth and death seven pages apart. Nine pages apart are panels of Tsukiko in a hospital bed and Kabuki in a hospital bed, both with head injuries and both in the same composition (pages 85 and 95). Kabuki becoming an adult and a Noh agent is condensed into four pages, before the narrative shifts to Kai. This means that Kabuki removing her mask and revealing her scar and Kai removing his mask and revealing his scar are only four pages apart as well. This spatial closeness, which is temporally quite distant, makes the connections clearer and works to intensify the coherence of Kabuki's backstory.

The second way that associations are made stronger is the inverse of closeness—distance. Tsukiko's grave turns up frequently in *Fear the Reaper* and *Circle of Blood* and infrequently in *Skin Deep* and *Metamorphosis*. While the narrative return of the grave is practically always in the same composition, what really matters is the panel where Kabuki lies dead on her mother's grave. As mentioned in chapter 1, this is a spatial rhyme, since the composition on pages 93 and 247 is identical. Furthermore, the splash page of 93 is repeated as a panel on page 220 (just as the splash page of 247 is repeated in *Dreams*). Whereas the closeness of pages generates intensity in terms of making the connections tighter, the distance of Kabuki dead on her mother's grave produces coherence. It marks who Kabuki is and associates her character with the narrative thematics of life-death-rebirth, as well as memory.

Rhythmic coherence, then, is both a matter of the intervals between different story lines and how they are made to intersect and a matter of literal spatial distance between events. The spatial closeness of events that are temporally distant or the constant return of specific panels emphasizes coherence and participates in the production of character coherence. Despite the fact that Kabuki undergoes major changes, rhythmic coherence becomes a device for maintaining character continuity.

However, coherence comes under pressure the further into the series we get, until there is essentially a complete change in Kabuki's identity in the collection *The Alchemy*, which suggests that Kabuki finally becomes Ukiko again and no longer serves the Noh agency. *The Alchemy* is a run of nine issues that concludes with Kabuki becoming a mother. The ending is suggestive of a circle, a spatial form that is less prominent in the collection than might be anticipated. Instead, boxes and squares dominate the page layouts more than in any previous collection. *The Alchemy* is also the collection that features the most mixed-media work from Mack. However, the most challenging part of *The Alchemy* is none of these devices. Instead, the story features far more nested boxes than earlier issues. This is true on a graphic level but also on a narrative level, where there are several frame breaks, something that had seldom appeared in *Kabuki*.

Frame breaks can occur in several different ways, and it is hardly unusual for comics to exploit the literal frame of the panel. For instance, Kabuki leans out of panel frames on pages 206 to 209 of *The Alchemy* while also explicitly referencing her being drawn (or not), as several panels present Kabuki as only partially drawn and Kabuki commenting on this. But there are also several instances of what Gérard Genette terms "metalepsis," the "intrusion by the extradiegetic narrator or narratee into the diegetic universe (or by diegetic characters into a metadiegetic universe, etc.)."[10] In the pages just mentioned, we see the literal story materials that Mack has used—script pages, notes, drawing tools, and so forth.

The clearest instance of metalepsis occurs at the end of part 3 and beginning of part 4 of *The Alchemy*. Kabuki is flying to the United States when another passenger asks if he can sit next to her. This man is David Mack. He not only looks like Mack but is also a writer, working on a script during the flight.[11] This encounter is metaleptical—one level of reality getting mixed up with another. Some frame breaks have happened before to some extent in *Kabuki* in relation to the Noh TV show that features fictionalized stories of the Noh agents' exploits. Mentioned as early as *Fear the Reaper*, this TV element is never really explored until *Scarab: Lost in Translation*, where Scarab often discusses the series and we get splash pages that depict scenes from the series.

Yet, this fictionalizing component is never pushed to the forefront the way it is in *The Alchemy*, especially when a double splash page of the outline of the airplane has excerpts from *Scarab: Lost in Translation* in circles around the plane's outline to indicate that Kabuki is watching the Noh TV series episode where all the agents fight each other. Here, the story mentioned first in *Scarab: Lost in Translation* is woven into Kabuki's story. Kabuki remarks on the dramatic irony of that episode as Mack maintains that this episode is good. Kabuki is aware of the dramatic irony of the fictionalized TV story line contrasted to her actual experience. This encounter has several metafictional winks that depend on publishing and industry trivia, such as Mack's character shifting from being drawn in a photorealistic style to a more cartoonish version with an exaggerated jawline as he claims to have worked as a detective in New York's Powers division. This is a reference to Brian Michael Bendis's square-jawed detective Christian Walker, with the added twist that Mack and Bendis are friends and have contributed forewords to each other's works.

More interesting than these knowing winks is the impact these frame shifts have on the spatial form of *The Alchemy*. It is as if breaking these fictional levels and playing around with nested narrative boxes has set Mack free from any illustration conventions and thereby pushed his style into graphic abstraction. Kabuki and Mack are reduced to iconic man-woman figures, and their dialogue runs in typed words on either side of them. Various graphic flourishes, such as more elaborate shadows that depict Kabuki as warrior, produce a highly varied page design. The abstraction of the design comes from the graphics having relatively little connection with the narrative as it unfolds. Once again dominated by splash pages without panels, *The Alchemy* also has few transitions to indicate temporal shifts or narrative shifts. Essentially, much of *The Alchemy* lacks a beat structure to introduce narrative change.

The collection feels like an introspection, something between a dream and a hallucination, where narrative progression is deemphasized, though still present. Kabuki appears to fumble toward a new identity. It is this quest toward a new identity that ushers in the spatial form of *The Alchemy* and its incessant use of boxes, or rather cubes, as alternative forms of panels. The encounter with Mack ends in part 4, and part 5 opens (on the pre-title page) with a watercolor painting of Kabuki in a paneled design with instructions to cut along the dotted line to produce a die and to roll it. This design dominates most pages in the fifth part and again in parts 8 and 9. At times the sides of the die work as panels, while at other times they are split panels for a watercolor painting of Kabuki.

The story progresses not so much in panel shifts but in captions that consist of letters exchanged between Akemi and Kabuki. Every letter begins with "Dear Kabuki friend" with Kabuki crossed out. This crossing out of the name suggests that Kabuki is trying to find a new identity or possibly discover who she really is. The instructions given at the beginning of part 5 are revealing in this respect, in two ways. First, the striking of her Noh name suggests a degree of randomness or lack of stability in Kabuki's identity, a difficulty in escaping who she was and has always been groomed to be. Second, from a spatial perspective, the painting of Kabuki fills up the die as a split panel, yet her hands, holding the Akemi Post-it, are painted outside the die design. At the risk of overinterpretation, the argument could be that Akemi is outside Kabuki's identity but also that Kabuki has to find her way without Akemi—if we do as instructed, we can never roll a result that includes Akemi. In other words, Kabuki will have to discover who she is without Akemi present. Alternatively, if the design is cut to allow for the Post-it, then Akemi would be folded inside the die and thus be part of Kabuki but not visible.

This instability argument is reinforced by the fact that the other prevalent page design is a splash page of figure outlines that depict Kabuki at various stages in her life—from little girl through different iterations as a Noh agent to being in the Control Corps to being disguised as the doctor. The last outline—who she is now—is done as either a dotted line or various other figures. While there is a certainty to Kabuki's past, there is no certainty to her future and no stable idea of who she will be.

This lack of coherence is also expressed through spatial form and page design. Listing all the different graphic styles and layouts in *The Alchemy* would be an almost insurmountable and futile task. Some of the more important designs include various diagrams that depict Kabuki as a robot, the dice designs, panels in the shape of a house, Kabuki as various creatures from *The Shy Creatures*. This last design needs to be discussed in some detail. Part 3 of *The Alchemy* opens with Kabuki reminiscing about her favorite childhood book, titled *The Shy Creatures*. This book is then depicted as inserts for half of part 3. It is about a shy girl who encounters all manner of fantastical beings—dragons, dinosaurs, cyclopes, aliens, and more. While there is some analogy between the shy girl and Kabuki and a notion that the fantastical creatures represent her life, the most significant aspect of the inserted book is the way that Kabuki thinks of that book as transformative. She is different upon having read it. And the subsequent pages are made of inserted photographs that depict Kabuki (this is the same model used in *Dreams*) cut into fragments, yet again underlining Kabuki's unstable identity.

Another aspect of *The Shy Creatures* needs to be mentioned. This pertains mostly to its publication history, although it also has a metafictional relation to *Kabuki*. The pages that make up *The Shy Creatures* were made specifically for *The Alchemy* as a visual means of exploring the themes of Kabuki in a different register. After *The Alchemy* was published, the Macmillan publishing house noticed that run of pages and agreed with Mack to publish it as its own children's book. Now, *The Shy Creatures* exists as a book in its own right, separate from the *Kabuki* story line. In a transmedia vocabulary, *The Shy Creatures* is a narrative extension—an object that first exists in the narrative world and is then later published (extended) into our world. In its own way *The Shy Creatures* does break the frame and in some metaphorical-literal way jumps off the page and makes its way as a book of its own. Genette would agree that this is an extension, though since nothing new is added in *The Shy Creatures* the book is as much an instance of excision—simply cut out of the initial text.[12] In either case, the move of *The Shy Creatures* from *Kabuki* to being its own thing is a case of frame-breaking and so remains also a case of metalepsis.

The expressive design and frame-breaking devices of *The Alchemy* all work together to blur and question notions of identity. *The Alchemy* collection is where the aspect of free-floating identities is pushed most to the foreground. The graphic style changes, the metaleptical shifts, the expressive use of other creatures as Kabuki, and much more together produce a highly varied and highly convoluted last installment in the series. Kabuki's reflection on her life and identity result in a highly self-reflexive work on the connection between art and life, art and identity.

The cubes are probably the most significant aspect of this reflexive component, due to their geometric configuration being used as a transformative vehicle. In part 8, Kabuki and Akemi sit and talk. The panels are laid out in the outline of a house, as if each panel were a room. The panel/house lines turn wavy and suddenly change into a cube that slowly unfolds across several pages, the inside of the cube containing a script for *Kabuki* stories. Akemi and Kabuki talk about turning her life into a comics story, what it should be called, and how it should be drawn. The cube closes again, and each panel is now a cube that unfolds, setting origami birds free, like the ones that Akemi used to make. They agree that the story should be called "Kabuki" and the first volume titled *Circle of Blood*. In part 9, a cube unfolds to become the cover to *Circle of Blood*, then changes back into a cube, back into a house (from part 8).

Then the house unfolds as a cube that matches an outline of Kabuki as a standing figure, then it reverts to a cube, origami birds, and then the final cube of Kabuki sitting, pregnant, and holding the Akemi Post-it.

All these geometric foldings and knots are highly complex, and the connection between each page shift is held together only by dialogue and character association. However, the geometric pattern of the cube-house-cube-house-cube-Kabuki does introduce a rhythm that also to some extent facilitates connection, even if this connection is far more abstract than what we have come across so far in *Kabuki*. Alongside the highly self-reflexive dialogue, what the boxes do is reinforce the various frames that are at play in *Kabuki*—Noh TV is referenced often, as a counterpoint to the story that Akemi and Kabuki are forging. More than anything, the shift between cube and house suggests an association with interiority and homeyness, associations that also link with concepts of identity. Kabuki is building her own house, her own story, and the dialogue with Akemi is a discussion of what form that story should have. This is rendered spatially as highly associative, if not exactly dreamlike. The rhythm that emerges in *The Alchemy* is not so much a narrative rhythm of progressivity but more a (self-)reflexive rhythm of Kabuki's identity. This rhythm cascades both forward and backward. Reading *The Alchemy* confronts the reader with the fact that all the earlier stories have been narrated from Kabuki's perspective. This is the metaleptical loop that runs in reverse. The more interesting rhythm is what we can call the "protentive" one—the one that runs into the future unknown. Kabuki is yet to become who she will be. A new rhythmic coherence is taking shape but left open. Kabuki will become Ukiko, whoever that is, but she is done with loops and repetitions, no longer caught up in the rhythm of the Noh but part of a new rhythm.

Coda: Rhythms in Comics

As I have shown, rhythms are a major part of how comics are structured. The rhythmic design of spatial arrangement is a crucial component for maintaining continuity and coherence throughout a long-running serial story. While the beat, the minimal narrative unit of change, remains, we can see how panels may also serve to either pause and extend duration or serve to emphasize an action or event within the unfolding of story.

Flow rhythms are often the dominant rhythms in narrative comics and facilitate causality and narrative progressivity through their clearly linked actions and events. Flashbacks and flashforwards are part of flow rhythms as long as their relation to the narrative rhythm is clear; narrative flow does not have to be linear. Turbulent rhythms complicate narrative unfolding and produce a distinctly different mood, more often associated with stoppage or blockage. Several instances of this are found in *Kabuki*, where the narrative becomes turbulent through dense spatial layouts or complicated panel shifts. Narrative turbulence is often associated, in *Kabuki*, with the internal pressures felt by Kabuki and the way that past and present intertwine as memories erupt.

One device that is often found in *Kabuki* is the looping of narrative time and events. Events' sequential position is undermined and open to revision or perspectival shifts that produce new narrative information. The same or similar events keep coming back, suggestive of narrative continuity, even as that continuity is revised. Loops in *Kabuki* are clearly related to the superhero comics' focus on origin stories, which are often repeated with some degree of variation. The variation of narrative loops in *Kabuki* serves to make the narrative progression more ambiguous and thus accentuates the narration as potentially unreliable.

Loops therefore lean up against rhythmic coherence, in that loops will challenge the rhythmic coherence that flow rhythms produce. Coherence works to suggest character continuity. Characters are made coherent through the rhythmic interaction of panels, pages, and sequences. The more well defined the narrative rhythms are, the clearer the characters will be. Turbulent rhythms may challenge character coherence, just as loops may disrupt whatever coherence has been produced so far. Yet, more than that, narrative rhythms work to assemble ideas of characters through their coherence. For *Kabuki*, we have seen how Kabuki's character is expressed through rhythmic coherence and then slowly altered through various forms of frame-breaking and metalepsis. It is the decoherence of these frame breaks that finally allows for a different coherence to begin to emerge. Spatial layout also expresses decoherence in *The Alchemy*, where many different spatial disruptions break the narrative frames. Only through this decoherence can Ukiko slowly reemerge from Kabuki.

Rhythms in comics are a spatial form in two ways. First, the spatial layouts of pages may in themselves produce a rhythm. Second, the sequential nature of the narrative progression may also produce a rhythm. In this manner, rhythm remains both a spatial form as I have generally discussed it throughout this book, but it also brings in the narrative structure and the way narrative progression and alternating story lines can produce opposing rhythms. There is a contrast, then, between rhyme and rhythm in that rhyme is concerned with non-narrative devices of linkage and repetition that reinforces thematic resonance and mood, while rhythm especially impacts the pacing of the narrative. In the same way, choreography is naturally associated with rhythms yet is more concerned with the expression of time than how the narrative is structured. Narrative flow is distinct from temporal flow in that narrative time is about sequence and causality, while temporal flows are about duration. Clearly affiliated, the two forms work in different ways. Finally, while perspective impacts narrative rhythm, perspective provides knowledge of the story, while narrative rhythm provides structure to the story.

Conclusion

It Opens at the Close

Kabuki exhibits the flexibility of spatial form. Spatial form establishes equivalences across the whole range of David Mack's collections and builds resonances across the serial story. *Kabuki* also shows how significant spatial forms are for comics, beyond the sequential structure that in many ways defines comics. These spatial forms are what finally come together to produce a spatial poetics of comics. No single work can ever hope to exhaust comics' aesthetic potentials, yet *Kabuki* showcases a foregrounding of spatial forms, indicating that comics are more than visual and sequential.

To say that comics are *more than* visual and sequential is not to deny that they *are* visual and sequential. The statement is intended only to reinforce the notion that there are many insights to be gained from thinking about comics' spatial form. The comics assemblage is a spatial structure that expresses time, mood, narrative, and a host of other aspects. This assemblage connects various forms that all express potentials for realization. While the realization is always singular on the level of the individual reader, the expressive forms can be studied and analyzed in their abstraction as potentials. This has been the goal of this book—to showcase how the expressive spatial forms of *Kabuki* work together as an assemblage of potentials. That is what an artwork is: an assemblage of expressive forms of potentials.

The spatial forms outlined here indicate the flexibility of comics as a medium; the spatial relations of the comics page and series afford many different permutations, as long as spatiality is taken seriously. As shown, spatial forms have implications for already-established critical terms (braiding, arthrology, narrative), where attention to spatial form reveals new aspects. Furthermore, exploring the ways that comics themselves articulate their stories reveals new opportunities, such as spatial rhymes or a more flexible way of understanding space-time relations as a choreography. Spatial form does not invalidate other approaches but expands and extends them.

Rhymes in comics are first and foremost spatial; while their equivalences depend on graphic matches and motifs, it is their spatial connections that form linkages. These linkages produce a degree of coherence that does not pertain to the narrative but instead functions to establish and intensify correspondences. This is also how rhymes are distinct from the idea of braiding. Braiding speaks to issues of repeating panels and the distance between those panels. Rhymes speak to the spatial equivalence that first of all goes beyond panels themselves to include motifs within panels. Second, rhymes are also invested in the spatial correspondence of placement on the page. That means that a spatial rhyme can produce linkage in two primary ways—first, by repeating a motif in different page locations, and second, by having similar motifs in the same page locations. These linkages often generate thematic resonances; in *Kabuki* this occurs especially in relation to Kabuki's past and the way that her past filters into her present.

The refrain works in a manner somewhat similar to the way linkages do, but it is a repetition without variation. We should be careful about exactly what this means. For example, Tsukiko's grave is repeated, even reproduced, many times across all the *Kabuki* collections, always without variation; the repetition itself *is* the variation. That is to say, just as Thierry Groensteen distinguishes between isometric and isotropic, a panel only signifies in relation to what is around it. Thus, any repetition varies in at least two ways. First, variation exists simply because it is a repetition and so bears with it the echo of having been encountered before. Second, since the panels and pages around the repeated panel are different, its significance necessarily shifts. In this way, the refrain is the productive tension between repetition and variation—never exactly one or the other but always located somewhere in between. For *Kabuki*, as we have seen, the significance keeps returning to Kabuki's mother and the repeated pattern of life-death-rebirth. Any refrain will always be particular to the story and so need not be related to a traumatic occurrence, even though the refrain has a long cultural history of being associated with death.

Choreography is my attempt at marking out a productive way of dealing with the problematic relationship of space and time in comics. While all critics and theorists agree that space is the way that comics can and must express time, there is no consensus as to how this expression works. Rather than seeing this as a problem to be solved, I prefer to consider it comics' greatest strength—an incredible flexibility in expressing time in so many different ways. Choreography seems to me to be the clearest way to express how this transformation of space into time occurs. All the different ways that comics artists have of connecting and linking panels and pages into sequences of time are deeply rooted in spatial relations, yet without any direct, simplistic correlation.

Kabuki is thoroughly enmeshed in the flexible ways that comics can express time. The vast majority of comics establish a flow of time by making clear shifts between panels and pages. Panel and page shifts that are clearly laid out and clearly indicate actions and events express a movement of time that flows. Causality and sequence are evident and linear, even if there are time shifts such as flashbacks and flashforwards. Once again, it is the spatial form of the panels and pages more than their visual expression that help produce this temporal flow. Graphic shifts may certainly participate in this temporal flow as well. Importantly, *Kabuki* also manipulates time in other ways. The folding of time is the primary way that *Kabuki* complicates temporal relations, and in much the same way that spatial rhymes reinforce thematic resonances and coherence, folding together multiple times into the same page or panel expresses the constant impingement of the past on the present.

Folding time is an unusual strategy that is not often found in comics, since it impedes the flow of time. For this reason, it is important to note that *Kabuki* almost always employs spatial rhymes and explicit narration to reinforce comprehension. We should keep in mind that time in comics is inherently plastic and may be layered in ways that can be quite dramatic. *Kabuki* employs this plasticity fully through the use of alterations in graphic style and collage layerings. Plasticity, for *Kabuki*, is used to suggest the subjective experience of time, contrasting the more extensive-objective flow of time with the intensive-subjective experience of time. In other words, time does not flow at just one speed but is tied to subjective experience, which again can be rendered spatially in comics, underscoring comics' flexibility in terms of time.

With the plunge into subjective experience, the idea of perspective as spatial form becomes a necessary discussion as well. Perspective speaks to both the literal spatial positioning of point of view in a panel, which is to say, the implied observer that any image necessarily must have, and also the more abstract spatial position of the narrator and focalizer. Where in the diegetic space are these narrating and focalizing agents placed? Although this may at first seem like less of a spatial form, there is no question that *Kabuki* holds several distinct diegetic levels and that the shifts between them are often quite subtle yet impact the level of reading.

First, the idea of narrator shifts is useful for those comics in which there are multiple narrators, especially when these narrators are also characters and even more so when, as in *Kabuki*, these narrators are actually the same character at different points in the narrative progression. The distance between different narrators may be expressed spatially, as it is in *Kabuki*, by employing different, overlapping forms. One instance of this is graphiation, where graphic styles shift depending on the narrative perspective. Although graphiation is a rare device in comics, *Kabuki* makes extensive use of it at various points in the collections and especially in relation to the mental strain that Kabuki experiences. Focalization is knotted together; several different perspectives exist within the same panel. This can be arranged spatially in comics and challenges the singularity of the narrating agent, which is necessarily multiple in *Kabuki*.

It is also spatial form that allows Mack to express the extreme mental strain that Kabuki experiences. Through his use of schizo-spatial focalization, multiple different perspectives are literally brought together into the same panel. Seeing the same event from different positions at the same time is of course a physical impossibility, but this spatial form can be articulated in comics, once again emphasizing the flexibility of the medium's expression. In this way, schizo-spatial focalization spatially arranges impossible and contradictory perspectives as the spatial equivalence of unreliable narration. Since multiple spatial positions cannot be held at the same time, which one is the more accurate or in what way should such panels be understood? While the use of such multiple spatial positions is unusual, it is not limited to *Kabuki*.

Narrative expression in comics is spatial in two ways—one is the arrangement of panels on pages and the other is the sequence of events that unfold. Once again, the first form is the more literal one, with the sequential form being somewhat more abstract. However, these two forms work together to produce a sense of narrative rhythm. Spatial arrangement enables comics to produce not just narrative beats but also two other significant aspects of rhythm—pause and emphasis. These three rhythmic functions are what produce either narrative flow or turbulence. For most comics, including *Kabuki*, narrative flow dominates the expression of actions and events that make up the story. The causal string of events that enable the realization of plot as story usually emerges as a flow, in which connections are intelligibly expressed and have an uncomplicated progression.

There are instances of narrative turbulence, however, in which the rhythmic functions of pause, beat, and emphasis are choreographed in a tension with narrative realization. In *Kabuki* narrative turbulence is most often associated with subtle shifts in focalization, with movement between external and internal experiences, associations, and memories. Once again, it is the spatial layout and panel shifts that make for narrative turbulence. Shifting between different perspectives can be done in a flowing narrative rhythm, but *Kabuki* accentuates the intensive aspects of Kabuki's experience by making the shifts less apparent and thereby disrupting narrative flow.

Much the same thing occurs with the narrative looping that *Kabuki* performs. Returning to and revising earlier events underscores the reliability of the narrating and focalizing agent, and readers thus return to a discussion of Kabuki's mental strain. Loop forms also connect to the contrasting of experience between two different characters, both of whom are positioned as narrating agents. This shift between different narrating agents that tell distinctly different versions of the same events brings us to the question of Kabuki's identity and the coherence that rhythms may instantiate.

Much of Kabuki's identity has been established by the spatial forms that I have discussed so far—the linkages and refrains of spatial rhymes, the complex choreographies of external and internal times, the perspectival shifts that produce different inflections of events. This has been the work of a rhythmic coherence that is productive of Kabuki as a character yet is also what brings about a major shift in her identity. Kabuki at the beginning of *Fear the Reaper* is not the same Kabuki we see in *The Alchemy*. Once again, this is expressed spatially as much as it is narratively. Rhyming, repetition, folding, knotting, and more are all forms that have produced the coherence of Kabuki. And then all of that stops. The spatial frame breaks that proliferate in *The Alchemy* are certainly done narratively through metaleptical encounters and events, but they are also accomplished spatially by folding and breaking the panels and pages of *The Alchemy*.

At the end of the series, we are able to see how its spatial form is laid out. The idea of retention, or memory, has been a constant thematic concern for Kabuki, for whom the past and the memories associated with that past often overwhelm her, leaving her identity fragile. This is a narrative concern that instantiates memory on a spatial level, through rhymes as well as perspectival, narrator, and graphic shifts that move between past and present and focus on their resonance. It is also a reader concern, in which the prevalence of repetition and variation places stringent demands on narrative memory and graphic recognition. We cannot read *Kabuki* without all of these different modes of retention. The comics' own spatial poetics signal this on every level.

And then, here at the end, it was all a story, not for reader enjoyment but a deliberately constructed sequence of events to bring Kabuki to this same place of realization—that everything that has happened before need not be part of who she will be. The end of *Kabuki*, unlike the rest of the series, is written in the future tense, figuratively speaking. This future tense is best understood as narrative protention. Narrative protention is often considered part of suspense and tension—unknown aspects of narrative resolution produce anticipation—yet this is not the case for *Kabuki*. There is no buildup to suspense at the end of *The Alchemy* but a winding down to a happy ever after, free from the strictures of the past. In a certain figurative sense, Kabuki dies and is reborn as Ukiko, yet this time Ukiko also literally gives birth, which seems to be what breaks the repetition impulse of the series. Now, there will be only variation, something new, something that is not known and not knowable.

The metaleptical retentive challenges that occur in *The Alchemy* effectively remove any notions of Kabuki having a coherent identity. Unlike the struggles she has in earlier collections, most markedly *Skin Deep* and *Metamorphosis*, in *The Alchemy* there is a celebration of this protentive identity still to come. Kabuki is finally free, open to the future, ready to become whomever she wants. That protentive promise cuts loose the retentive memories of her past life, a life that is no more than a story, to erase her old self and allow her to find a new life.

This narrative conclusion is not in itself particularly unusual; happy endings are entirely typical, and having the protagonist begin a new, different life is certainly also conventional for many stories. Comics are often serial in nature, however; stories continue more often than they conclude. Closure in comics is less typical not because of their medium but rather as a result of the vagaries of publishing, whether in the United States or Europe. Narrative space is generally kept open, even if only for the possibility of new stories. This is not the case for *Kabuki*, and *The Alchemy* serves as what Jason Mittell has referred to as a "conclusion"—"a sense of finality and resolution."[1] Although there are many differences between American TV and American comics, the notion that success constitutes an infinite middle with no end is common for both.

Kabuki has itself expanded its middle with collections such as *Dreams* that do not directly progress the narrative further but instead give more information about already known story events. The spin-offs *Masks of the Noh* and especially *Scarab: Lost in Translation* also provide more of this expanded middle, while *Scarab* also opens up the narrative space to focus on minor characters. Both of these spin-offs have clear endings, with no more narrative space available for them. One could imagine new spin-offs for the other Noh agents, however.

What is more unusual is that the closure of *Kabuki*'s narrative space is expressed as the opening of a new narrative space that is not continuous with the one we have just experienced. Again, we find such narrative openings easily enough in several other comics, such as *The Wicked + The Divine* (Kieron Gillen and Jamie McKelvie, 2014–19), which explicitly states at its end this opportunity for new narrative space. *Blankets* (Craig Thompson, 2003) also shifts from one narrative space to a more open narrative space at its end, with Craig finding peace with his parents and making peace with the loss of his first love. The title and reference to blankets carry several significations from the story, including blankets of white snow parallel to pages as yet unwritten (a motif possibly borrowed from James Joyce's *Dubliners*). The confluence of autobiographical comics and the common structure of the bildungsroman found in many comics also point to this shift in narrative space at the end of a comics arc.[2] *Kabuki* is not autobiographical but does carry many traces of autobiographical elements, and certainly Ukiko/Kabuki's story is very much a story of formation.

This formation story or bildungsroman occurs as the logic of the frame break and is why this break is, in fact, a necessity for the story to conclude. Kabuki has had one narrative pace, which has been full of repetitions and returns of her mother and her past; Ukiko now takes over, no longer as the child that became Kabuki but as the Kabuki that has become a mother. From a narrative perspective, we can think of the ending of *The Alchemy* and the conclusion of *Kabuki* as aperture, as opposed to closure. Narrative aperture, like narrative closure, is another spatial form, even if it is figurative rather than literal. But the form of aperture, or simply opening, is of course also paradoxical, which is why it is connected, in this case, with a frame break. For *Kabuki* does not open here; it closes. One might be tempted to use a spatial expression from a different popular story: "It opens at the close," from the *Harry Potter* franchise.

The literal spatial rearrangements that make up the majority of *The Alchemy* also make up the closure of the series as a whole: boxes, cubes, houses that fold together and unfold, the metalepsis that reconfigures the narrative as a story told from Kabuki's perspective to escape the confines of that story. In a sense, this is a kind of narrative Escher effect: what we thought was arranged in one way is shown to be arranged in a different manner. Such a revision is somewhat rare, akin to a character waking up after a dream. And yet, *The Alchemy* does not have the quality of a dream, a texture that would be more associated with *Skin Deep* and parts of *Metamorphosis*. *The Alchemy* simply feels like a release, a letting go of one's past in favor of one's future. There is little melancholy at the end, more an unclenching into a better state of being. Aperture becomes a spatial form of open possibilities, rather than a static fixture. It is with those open possibilities that we leave Ukiko in an as-yet-unformed future.

What *Kabuki* shows us is that space is dynamic, not static. Space should be conceived as a space of potentials, open to different realizations. The series shows how comics' use of spatial form enables an almost limitless arrangement of panel composition and page layout and how the interaction between composition and structure is flexible. This interaction enables many different spatial forms to emerge, and *Kabuki* only scratches the surface of what the comics medium is able to do.

A spatial poetics of comics does not deny the visual aspect of comics, does not deny the interplay between word and image, does not deny the narrative function of panel, page, and series sequentiality. What a spatial poetics does do is emphasize other expressions that pertain to connections and correspondences. These connections express a different, complementary, but no less significant logic than that of sequential structure. While it may seem counterintuitive, a spatial poetics emphasizes flows and transformations more than stability and structure. This goes back to the insistence that space is dynamic, not static. While this dynamic nature of space is of course only realized by the reader, it is the spatial forms that afford these potentials for realization. *Kabuki*'s space of potentials is helpful as a way of informing an analytical understanding of the spatial poetics of all comics, since these spatial potentials are so foregrounded in the series.

NOTES

INTRODUCTION

1. Mikkonen, *Narratology of Comic Art*, 12.
2. Beaty, *Comics versus Art*, 36ff.
3. For more on this, see Meskin, "Defining Comics?"
4. Groensteen, *System of Comics*, 18.
5. Bukatman, *Hellboy's World*, loc. 2074.
6. Lavin, "Women in Comic Books," 98.
7. Shively, "*Bakufu* versus *Kabuki*," 36.
8. Mack, *Kabuki Omnibus*, 1:318.
9. Peeters, "Four Conceptions of the Page," 3.
10. Groensteen, *System of Comics*, 6.
11. Kukkonen, *Studying Comics and Graphic Novels*, 7.
12. Baetens and Frey, *Graphic Novel*, 8.
13. Fresnault-Deruelle, "From Linear to Tabular," 129.
14. Hatfield quoted in Hague, *Comics and the Senses*, 22.
15. Cohn, *Visual Language of Comics*, 17ff.
16. Mikkonen, *Narratology of Comic Art*, 40; Groensteen, *System of Comics*, 112.
17. Groensteen, *System of Comics*, 21.
18. Bukatman, *Hellboy's World*, loc. 244.
19. McCloud, *Understanding Comics*, 67 (original emphasis).
20. Groensteen, *System of Comics*, 60.
21. Cortsen, "Comics as Assemblage," 110.
22. Frank, *Idea of Spatial Form*, 10. ("Spatial Form in Modern Literature" is reprinted as the first chapter in Frank's *The Idea of Spatial Form*.)
23. Mitchell, "Spatial Form in Literature," 542.
24. Mitchell, "Spatial Form in Literature," 543.
25. Frank, *Idea of Spatial Form*, 12.
26. DeLanda, *Intensive Science and Virtual Philosophy*, 27 (original emphasis).
27. DeLanda, *Intensive Science and Virtual Philosophy*, 27 (original emphasis).
28. Bal, "Narration and Focalization," 277.

29. See, for instance, Bal, *Narratology*, 89ff.
30. Genette, *Narrative Discourse*, 234ff.

1. SPATIAL RHYMES

1. Cohn, "Limits of Time and Transitions," 137.
2. Fresnault-Deruelle, "From Linear to Tabular," 133.
3. Groensteen, *System of Comics*, 148. Groensteen also mentions rhyme in his 2016 article "The Art of Braiding: A Clarification," but here he also does not develop the idea and only quotes himself verbatim. I leave it up to the reader to decide if this is a citational practice or an insistence.
4. Gavaler, *Comics Form*, 87.
5. Attridge, *Poetic Rhythm*, 10.
6. Groensteen, *System of Comics*, 158.
7. Groensteen, *System of Comics*, 147.
8. McCloud, *Understanding Comics*, 70–72; Groensteen, *System of Comics*, 18.
9. Baetens and Frey, *Graphic Novel*, 106.
10. Rimmon-Kenan, "Paradoxical Status of Repetition," 153.
11. Motte, "Work of Mourning," 57–58.
12. A quick note about this interview as a recap. Although in many ways this opening chapter can be seen as providing a recapping function for new readers, *Metamorphosis* is of course a new collection. However, it is hard to imagine new readers beginning with this collection, except possibly by mistake. The collection is clearly marked as part of a longer series. The repetition must be regarded as an aesthetic motivation.
13. Pagello, "'Origin Story' Is the Only Story," 729.

2. CHOREOGRAPHIES

1. McCloud, *Understanding Comics*, 100.
2. Groensteen, *System of Comics*, 35, 40.
3. Chute and DeKoven, "Introduction: Graphic Narrative," 769. Hillary Chute employs the term "boxes of time" in her book *Graphic Women*, 6.
4. Round, "Visual Perspective and Narrative Voice in Comics," 323.
5. Chute, "Comics as Literature?," 454.
6. McCloud, *Understanding Comics*, 70.
7. Mack's word order is itself interesting. Why is it a "frightened sea of faces," when one would assume that the faces are what express

fright? Presumably it is because this is a collective feeling, expressed collectively.
8. McCloud discusses the idea of timelessness as a function of wordless panels, especially if they bleed to the edge. McCloud, *Understanding Comics*, 101–2.
9. Cohn, "Limits of Time and Transitions," 139.
10. Cohn, "Limits of Time and Transitions," 136.
11. Cohn, "Limits of Time and Transitions," 134; Cohn, "Visual Lexicon," 43.
12. Round, "Visual Perspective and Narrative Voice in Comics," 323.
13. Fresnault-Deruelle, "From Linear to Tabular," 121.
14. Gunning, "Art of Succession," 41
15. I say "may," since a reader in the grip of the action may well skip past most of the visual detail to get at the story.
16. Chute, "Comics as Literature?," 455.
17. Cohn, "Limits of Time and Transitions," 133.
18. Chute, "Comics as Literature?," 453.
19. Hague, "Folding, Cutting, Reassembling," 181, discusses this distinction of time in comics.
20. Groensteen, *System of Comics*, 53, 50, respectively.
21. Bukatman, *Hellboy's World*, loc. 1984. He takes the term from Noël Burch's term "pillow-shot," which he developed to articulate film director Ozu Yasujiro's aesthetics and introduced in *To the Distant Observer*.
22. Hatfield, *Alternative Comics*, 48.
23. Hatfield, *Alternative Comics*, 58.
24. Sacco, *Footnotes in Gaza*, 235.
25. Morrison and Burnham, *Nameless*, 116.

3. PERSPECTIVES

1. This is Gérard Genette's classic distinction; see Genette, *Narrative Discourse*, 244–45.
2. Mikkonen, "Presenting Minds in Graphic Narratives," 308.
3. Kukkonen, *Contemporary Comics Storytelling*, 33.
4. Plenty of comics accentuate this relation and have an unknown narrator whose identity is revealed only gradually or at the end. One classic example is Alan Moore and Eddie Campbell's *From Hell* (1999).
5. Gaudreault, *From Plato to Lumière*, 7, 69.
6. Groensteen, *Comics and Narration*, 86.
7. Mikkonen, *Narratology of Comic Art*, 86.

8. Rimmon-Kenan, *Narrative Fiction*, 69.
9. Kukkonen, *Studying Comics and Graphic Novels*, 45.
10. Bordwell, *Narration in the Fiction Film*, 58.
11. Mikkonen, *Narratology of Comic Art*, 111.
12. Mikkonen, *Narratology of Comic Art*, 119, 120.
13. Mikkonen, *Narratology of Comic Art*, 120.
14. Kukkonen, *Contemporary Comics Storytelling*, 151–53.
15. Rimmon-Kenan, *Narrative Fiction*, 79–83.
16. Chatman, *Story and Discourse*, 96ff.
17. The captions are also handwritten, as is almost all lettering in comics, but as is so often the case the lettering is done in printed handwriting or in computer font that resembles printed handwriting, thereby making the text as neutral and standardized as possible.
18. Horstkotte and Pedri, "Focalization in Graphic Narrative," 336.
19. Kukkonen, *Contemporary Comics Storytelling*, 33.
20. Kukkonen, *Studying Comics and Graphic Novels*, 45.
21. The idea of nontrivial effort comes from Espen Aarseth and ergodic literature, developed in his 1997 book *Cybertext: Perspectives on Ergodic Literature*. However, *Kabuki* is not an example of ergodic literature, so I will not pursue this idea here.
22. Deleuze and Guattari, *Anti-Oedipus*, 7.
23. Deleuze and Guattari, *Anti-Oedipus*, 7.
24. Hague, *Comics and the Senses*, 113.

4. RHYTHMS

1. Groensteen, *System of Comics*, 45.
2. Groensteen, *Comics and Narration*, 149.
3. Kochalka, *Horrible Truth about Comics*, 15.
4. Several scholars term this form of alternation "parallel editing," modeled after cinematic editing terminology, including continuity editing. See, for instance, Kukkonen, *Studying Comics and Graphic Novels*. Although this model has many pedagogical strengths, including being quite intuitive, comics do not really follow a similar organization. Part of this chapter is meant to propose a different model for narrative progression.
5. In the terminology of the preceding chapter, these surveillance TV panels represent a narrator shift.
6. Groensteen, *Comics and Narration*, 135.
7. Groensteen, *Comics and Narration*, 149.
8. For more on this phenomenon, see Friedenthal, *Retcon Game*.

9. Friedenthal, *Retcon Game*, 7.
10. Genette, *Narrative Discourse*, 234–35.
11. Anyone who knows about Mack's writing process, documented in various collections, knows that he often writes during his travels.
12. Genette, *Palimpsests*, 229.

CONCLUSION

1. Mittell, *Complex TV*, 321.
2. For more on the bildungsroman and comics, see Fantasia, "Paterian *Bildungsroman* Reenvisioned"; Schwarz and Crenshaw, "Old Media, New Media"; and Earle, "*My Friend Dahmer.*"

BIBLIOGRAPHY

Attridge, Derek. *Poetic Rhythm: An Introduction*. Cambridge: Cambridge University Press, 1995.

Baetens, Jan, and Hugo Frey. *The Graphic Novel: An Introduction*. Cambridge: Cambridge University Press, 2014.

Bal, Mieke. "Narration and Focalization." In *Narrative Theory: Critical Concepts in Literary and Cultural Studies*, edited by Mieke Bal, 263–96. London: Routledge, 2004.

——— . *Narratology: Introduction to the Theory of Narrative*. 4th ed. Toronto: University of Toronto Press, 2017.

Beaty, Bart. *Comics versus Art*. Toronto: University of Toronto Press, 2012.

Bechdel, Alison. *Fun Home: A Family Tragicomic*. Boston: Mariner Books, 2007.

Bordwell, David. *Narration in the Fiction Film*. Madison: University of Wisconsin Press, 1985.

Bukatman, Scott. *Hellboy's World: Comics and Monsters on the Margins*. Berkeley: University of California Press, 2016. Kindle.

Burch, Noël. *To the Distant Observer: Form and Meaning in the Japanese Cinema*. Revised and edited by Annette Michelson. Berkeley: University of California Press, 1979.

Chatman, Seymour. *Story and Discourse: Narrative Structure in Fiction and Film*. Ithaca: Cornell University Press, 1980.

Chute, Hillary. "Comics as Literature? Reading Graphic Narrative." *Publications of the Modern Language Association of America* 123, no. 2 (2008): 452–65.

Chute, Hillary L. *Graphic Women: Life Narrative and Contemporary Comics*. New York: Columbia University Press, 2010.

Chute, Hillary L., and Marianne DeKoven. "Introduction: Graphic Narrative." *Modern Fiction Studies* 52, no. 4 (2006): 767–82.

Cohn, Neil. "The Limits of Time and Transitions: Challenges to Theories of Sequential Image Comprehension." *Studies in Comics* 1, no. 1 (2010): 127–47.

——— . *The Visual Language of Comics: Introduction to the Structure and Cognition of Sequential Images*. London: Bloomsbury, 2013.

———. "A Visual Lexicon." *Public Journal of Semiotics* 1, no. 1 (2007): 35–56.

Cortsen, Rikke Platz. "Comics as Assemblage: How Spatio-Temporality in Comics Is Constructed." Doctoral diss., Copenhagen University, 2012.

DeLanda, Manuel. *Intensive Science and Virtual Philosophy*. London: Continuum, 2002.

Deleuze, Gilles, and Félix Guattari. *Anti-Oedipus: Capitalism and Schizophrenia*. Translated by Robert Hurley, Mark Seem, and Helen R. Lane. Minneapolis: University of Minnesota Press, 1983.

Earle, Harriet E. H. "*My Friend Dahmer*: The Comic as *Bildungsroman*." *Journal of Graphic Novels and Comics* 5, no. 4 (2014): 429–40.

Fantasia, Annette. "The Paterian *Bildungsroman* Reenvisioned: 'Brain Building' in Alison Bechdel's *Fun Home: A Family Tragicomic*." *Criticism* 53, no. 1 (2011): 83–97.

Frank, Joseph. *The Idea of Spatial Form*. New Brunswick NJ: Rutgers University Press, 1991.

Fresnault-Deruelle, Pierre. "From Linear to Tabular." In *The French Comics Theory Reader*, edited by Ann Miller and Bart Beaty, 121–38. Leuven, Belgium: Leuven University Press, 2014.

Friedenthal, Andrew. *Retcon Game: Retroactive Continuity and the Hyperlinking of America*. Jackson: University Press Mississippi, 2017.

Gaudreault, André. *From Plato to Lumière: Narration and Monstration in Literature and Cinema*. Toronto: University of Toronto Press, 2009.

Gavaler, Chris. *The Comics Form: The Art of Sequenced Images*. London: Bloomsbury, 2022.

Genette, Gérard. *Narrative Discourse: An Essay in Method*. Translated by Jane E. Lewin. Ithaca: Cornell University Press, 1983.

———. *Palimpsests: Literature in the Second Degree*. Translated by Channa Newman and Claude Dubinsky. Lincoln: University of Nebraska Press, 1997.

Groensteen, Thierry. *Comics and Narration*. Translated by Ann Miller. Jackson: University Press of Mississippi, 2013.

———. *The System of Comics*. Translated by Bart Beaty and Nick Nguyen. Jackson: University Press of Mississippi, 2007.

Gunning, Tom. "The Art of Succession: Reading, Writing, and Watching Comics." *Critical Inquiry* 40, no. 3 (2014): 36–51.

Hague, Ian. *Comics and the Senses: A Multisensory Approach to Comics and Graphic Novels*. New York: Routledge, 2014.

———. "Folding, Cutting, Reassembling: Materializing Trauma and Memory in Comics." In *Documenting Trauma in Comics: Traumatic Pasts, Embodied Histories, and Graphic Reportage*, edited by Dominic Davies and Candida Rifkind, 179–97. Cham, Switzerland: Palgrave Macmillan, 2020.

Hatfield, Charles. *Alternative Comics: An Emerging Literature*. Jackson: University Press of Mississippi, 2009.

Horstkotte, Silke, and Nancy Pedri. "Focalization in Graphic Narrative." *Narrative* 19, no. 3 (2011): 330–57.

Kochalka, James. *The Horrible Truth about Comics*. Cupertino CA: Alternative Comics, 1999.

Kukkonen, Karin. *Contemporary Comics Storytelling*. Lincoln: University of Nebraska Press, 2013.

———. *Studying Comics and Graphic Novels*. Chichester, UK: John Wiley & Sons, 2013.

Lavin, Michael R. "Women in Comic Books." *Serials Review* 24, no. 2 (1998): 93–100.

Lorente, Joaquín Martínez. "Blurring Focalization: Psychological Expansions of Point of View and Modality." *Revista Alicantina de Estudios Ingleses*, no. 9 (1996): 63–89.

Mack, David. *Kabuki Omnibus*. 4 vols. Milwaukie OR: Dark Horse Books, 2019–21.

Matz and Luc Jacamon. *The Killer*. Los Angeles CA: Archaia, 2018.

McCloud, Scott. *Understanding Comics: The Invisible Art*. New York: HarperCollins, 1993.

Meskin, Aaron. "Defining Comics?" *Journal of Aesthetics and Art Criticism* 65, no. 4 (2007): 369–79.

Mikkonen, Kai. *The Narratology of Comic Art*. New York: Routledge, 2017.

———. "Presenting Minds in Graphic Narratives." *Partial Answers: Journal of Literature and the History of Ideas* 6, no. 2 (2008): 301–21.

Mitchell, W. J. T. "Spatial Form in Literature: Toward a General Theory." *Critical Inquiry* 6, no. 3 (1980): 539–67.

Mittell, Jason. *Complex TV: The Poetics of Contemporary Television Storytelling*. New York: New York University Press, 2015.

Moon, Fábio, and Gabriel Bá. *Daytripper*. New York: DC Comics, 2010.

Morrison, Grant, and Chris Burnham. *Nameless*. Berkeley CA: Image Comics, 2016.

Motte, Warren. "The Work of Mourning." *Yale French Studies*, no. 105 (2004): 56–71.

Pagello, Federico. "The 'Origin Story' Is the Only Story: Seriality and Temporality in Superhero Fiction from Comics to Post-Television." *Quarterly Review of Film and Video* 34, no. 8 (2017): 725–45.

Peeters, Benoît. "Four Conceptions of the Page." *ImageTexT: Interdisciplinary Comics Studies* 3, no. 3 (2007): 41–60.

Remender, Rick. *Venom*. New York: Marvel Comics, 2015.

Rimmon-Kenan, Shlomith. *Narrative Fiction: Contemporary Poetics*. 2nd ed. London: Routledge, 2002.

———. "The Paradoxical Status of Repetition." *Poetics Today* 1, no. 4 (1980): 151–59.

Round, Julia. "Visual Perspective and Narrative Voice in Comics." *International Journal of Comic Art* 9, no. 3 (2007): 316–29.

Sacco, Joe. *Footnotes in Gaza*. London: Jonathan Cape, 2009.

Schwarz, Gretchen, and Christina Crenshaw. "Old Media, New Media: The Graphic Novel as *Bildungsroman*." *Journal of Media Literacy Education* 3, no. 1 (2011): 47–53.

Shively, Donald H. "*Bakufu* versus *Kabuki*." In *A Kabuki Reader: History and Performance*, edited by Samuel L. Leiter, 33–59. Armonk NY: M. E. Sharpe, 2002.

Vaughn, Sarah, and Jonathan Luna. *Alex + Ada*. Vol. 1. Berkeley CA: Image Comics, 2014.

INDEX

analepsis, 49
arthrology, 17
assemblage, 18–19, 21, 26, 27, 35, 38, 39, 42–43, 51, 68, 69; and spatial arrangement, 14, 20, 50, 105, 120, 161

braiding, 26, 29, 33, 35, 38, 50, 144, 162
breakdown, page, 37, 115, 134

choreography, 22, 53, 59, 62, 67–68, 69, 74, 77, 81, 82, 83–84, 120, 121, 134, 158, 162, 163
coherence, 32, 35, 40, 59, 66, 123, 145, 162, 164; and character, 150, 158; and rhythm, 145–50, 154, 156, 158, 167; and story, 31, 32, 39, 140
comics: definition of, 3; dimensions of, 14; as network, 17; space of possibilities in, 20; spatial arrangement of, 14, 20, 50, 105, 120, 161; time in, 52, 56, 58, 60, 65, 69. *See also* assemblage
composition, 13, 22, 32, 55–56, 90, 133, 149–50
configuration, 16
correspondence, 25, 30, 162

flow, 31, 52, 62, 123; movement, 69; narrative, 62, 72, 75, 79, 89, 126, 129, 130, 131, 132, 133, 137, 140, 145, 157, 159, 166; reading, 21, 30, 89, 102, 114, 116, 127, 133; spatial, 31, 61, 83; temporal, 59, 60, 61, 62, 68, 69, 71, 72, 82, 99, 145, 158, 159, 164
focalization, 4, 22, 49, 76, 77, 80, 85, 96, 97, 99, 119, 120, 139, 140, 142, 143, 144, 166; knotting, 105–7, 109, 110, 111, 112, 121, 165; schizo-spatial, 112, 113, 114, 116, 117, 119, 121, 130, 165
folding, 52, 65, 67–68, 82–83, 94, 164
frame breaks, 151

graphiation, 85, 91–92, 94, 103, 120, 165
graphic style, 11, 12, 22, 30, 31, 44, 77, 79, 80, 85, 89, 91, 92, 94, 95, 96, 100, 101, 102, 103, 105, 110, 111, 113, 117, 120, 138, 142, 155, 164, 165
gridding, 77, 102–3, 133–34
gutter, 18

iconic solidarity, 17
isometric, 163
isotropic, 163

Kabuki, summary of, 4–11
knotting, 105, 107, 112, 121

leitmotif, 41
linear-tabular, 59, 61, 62, 65, 67, 68, 77, 82, 120, 122, 127, 129
linkage, 21, 22, 25, 29, 32, 33, 34, 35, 36, 37, 38, 40, 43, 46, 49, 50, 51, 78, 149, 158, 162, 167
loops, 132, 138, 139, 140, 143, 144, 156, 157, 158, 166

Mack, David, 4
metalepsis, 151
motif, 3, 17, 25, 34, 38, 49; graphic, 25, 26, 27, 30, 31, 32, 34, 35, 41, 50, 162; narrative, 5, 38, 39, 132; rhyming, 26, 29, 31, 33, 36, 43, 50, 58
mourning, 39–40, 42

narration, 22, 34, 65, 76, 85, 86, 88, 89, 90, 91, 105, 114, 118, 119, 120, 121, 157, 164; agent of, 86, 91; and enunciation, 87, 91; and graphiation, 91, 92, 94, 96; heterodiegetic, 86; homodiegetic, 86
narrative, 3, 14, 20, 29, 53; aperture, 170; closure, 170; emphasis, 26; flow, 72, 75, 79, 89, 126, 129, 130, 131, 132, 133, 137, 157, 166; loops, 138, 140; motivation, 45, 137; time, 53, 57, 58, 63, 65, 73, 134, 158; turbulence, 134, 135, 157, 166
narrator, 86, 91, 97, 107, 109, 120; heterodiegetic, 86; homodiegetic, 86; and protention, 123; and retention, 123; shifts, 86, 90, 91, 92, 93, 95, 96, 105, 120, 121, 132, 165, 167
network, comics as, 17

perspective, 22, 57, 61, 76, 85, 86, 96, 97, 99, 103, 107, 109, 115, 116, 120, 121, 138, 139, 153, 156, 159, 164, 165
plasticity, 52, 69, 76, 81, 83, 164
point of view, 85
positioning, 4, 22, 85, 113, 115, 116, 121, 164
potentials, 57, 68, 119, 171
prolepsis, 49

refrain, 25, 29, 38–41, 42, 43, 44, 45, 46, 48, 49, 50, 139, 162, 163, 167
repetition, 25, 26, 37, 38, 40, 41, 43, 45, 46, 47, 49, 50, 126, 158, 162, 163, 167
resemblance, 25, 36
rhyme, 4, 25, 26, 27, 30, 31, 32, 46, 48, 49, 50, 58, 65, 66, 67, 69, 74, 78, 81, 88, 148, 149, 150, 158, 162, 164, 167
rhythm, 4, 22, 61, 103, 123, 125, 130, 157; coherence of, 123, 145, 146, 147, 150, 158, 167; emphasis of, 126, 127, 129; and loops, 132; narrative, 132, 133, 140, 143, 144, 149, 166; and pauses, 126; and space, 123, 144; and turbulence, 134, 135, 136, 137, 139

sequence, 19, 22, 29, 35
series, 17, 18, 21
space, 1, 13, 39; extensive, 20; intensive, 21, 30, 37; narrative, 41, 46, 106, 168–69; possibilities of, 20; rhyme and, 26, 27
spatial form, 1, 4, 14, 19, 21
spatial poetics, 3, 13, 16–17, 20, 171
spatio-topical system, 13
surface, 77, 80

temporal map, 66–67
time, 16, 22, 42, 51, 52, 55, 56, 57, 162; choreography of, 21, 67, 81, 163; compression of, 58; flow of, 60, 61, 62, 82, 131, 163; folding of, 65, 66, 73, 80, 81, 82, 164; plasticity of, 69, 72, 73, 76, 81; shifts, 56, 57, 59, 68, 75, 76, 79, 81, 82, 87, 111, 164

transitions, 19, 35, 54, 81, 124
turbulence, 134, 166

variation, 21, 35, 43, 44, 46, 47, 90, 91, 111, 157, 162, 163, 167, 168

In the Encapsulations: Critical Comics Studies series

Storytelling in "Kabuki": An Exploration of Spatial Poetics of Comics
Steen Ledet Christiansen

Aquaman and the War against Oceans: Comics Activism and Allegory in the Anthropocene
Ryan Poll

The New Nancy: Flexible and Relatable Daily Comics in the Twenty-First Century
Jeff Karnicky

To order or obtain more information on these or other University of Nebraska Press titles, visit nebraskapress.unl.edu.

www.ingramcontent.com/pod-product-compliance
Lightning Source LLC
Chambersburg PA
CBHW020423230426
43663CB00007BA/1289